Praise for CRI  oals

"She is a master at weaving relevant stories and concepts together and, at the same time, making everyone in the audience feel like she's the truth-speaking best friend they need."

—Jessica Bufkin, FinCon Director of Events

"Bernadette is for the everyday person—to maximize their time, finances, and resources. She's so dang practical."

—Eugene Robinson, TV host and NFL player

"Bernadette's lived experience adds depth and relatability to her approach, making her an invaluable resource for anyone looking to improve their financial situation."

—Stefanie Gonzales, Women's Wealth Effect

"Bernadette brings joy to finance in a way that most people need—and most people don't even imagine is possible."

—Yinka Ewuola, founder of the Cashflow Accelerator

"Bernadette has been such a blessing in my life. She's always doing something for others. She is so smart and wise beyond her years and thinks way outside the common way of thinking."

—Carla Carlisle, mental health advocate and TEDx speaker

"Bernadette helped me unlock the golden handcuffs of big banking. She truly cares and brings a refreshing and relatable style to personal finance that's a breath of fresh air. Who knew budgets and finances could be fun? I didn't—until I met Bernadette!"

—Megan Spivey, founder of Career Outfitters

"Following Bernadette's principles, I have paid off over $50,000 of credit card debt, quit my job, and launched a luxury residential interior design business in Charlotte, North Carolina. Thanks to Bernadette, I have generated over a million dollars in revenue—and am doing it debt-free!"

—Marie Matthews, luxury interior designer

BERNADETTE JOY

CRUSH YOUR MONEY GOALS®

25 SMART MONEY HABITS
to Save, Invest, and Fast-Track
Your Financial Freedom

Adams Media
New York   London   Toronto   Sydney   New Delhi

Adams Media
An Imprint of Simon & Schuster, LLC
100 Technology Center Drive
Stoughton, Massachusetts 02072

First Adams Media trade paperback edition December 2024

ADAMS MEDIA and colophon are registered trademarks of Simon & Schuster, LLC.

Simon & Schuster: Celebrating 100 Years of Publishing in 2024

For information about special discounts for bulk purchases, please contact Simon & Schuster Special Sales at 1-866-506-1949 or business@simonandschuster.com.

The Simon & Schuster Speakers Bureau can bring authors to your live event. For more information or to book an event, contact the Simon & Schuster Speakers Bureau at 1-866-248-3049 or visit our website at www.simonspeakers.com.

Interior design by Colleen Cunningham

Manufactured in the United States of America

1 2024

Library of Congress Cataloging-in-Publication Data has been applied for.

ISBN 978-1-5072-2263-8
ISBN 978-1-5072-2264-5 (ebook)

*Dedicated to the past and future members of CRUSH Bootcamp.
You deserve all the freedom and joy you've gifted me over the years.*

*And to the first and forever CRUSH Bootcamp member, AJ—
freedom would be meaningless without you. I'm forever grateful.*

Contents

Preface

Hey, hey, my new friend in financial freedom! Ready to CRUSH your money goals? I'm Bernadette, your millionaire mentor and the rich auntie you didn't know you needed until this very moment. I firmly believe that this book will not only help you learn all the things you wish someone had taught you about money when you were growing up, but also show you how to build smart money habits that will last your lifetime. Like you, I started my own financial journey by searching for a better way to handle my money. In 2016, I found myself crying on the floor of my office when I realized I had more than $300,000 in debt between my student loans, mortgages, and everyday expenses, and my only plan was to "work hard."

My father had nine children in total, seven from his first marriage and two in his second marriage. I was the eighth of this complicated Filipino immigrant family, so the only way I learned to manage money was just that—work hard. Don't have enough money? Work harder. Have debt and are stressed out to the max? You're not working hard enough. I thought, *There must be a better way. This life can't be it.* So I researched every piece of personal finance advice I could find online. Some if it was useful, but much of it felt outdated, out of touch, and out of reach. This is the book I wish had existed when I was searching for solutions, much as you are right now.

As I started paying off $72,000 in student loans in 2016, I shared my journey online by sharing pictures of sticky notes on my refrigerator that tracked my debt dwindling down until I finished my last student loan payment less than a year after I started aggressively paying toward it.

The responses flooded into my inbox, prompting requests for countless coffee dates to explain my approach. Eventually there came a point where I was going on too many coffee dates (and I don't even drink coffee), and I started feeling like a broken record, repeating the same story over and over again.

One night, I joked to my husband, AJ, "One day, I'll just record my response to the same questions and instead of going to these 'pick my brain' sessions, I'll just send them the recording." He responded, "You know that's called a podcast, right?" So, I must credit AJ with the idea—recording my student loan payoff tips as a podcast starting in 2018. Originally titled *F*** This Debt*, the podcast was rebranded as *CRUSH This Debt* after I received a piece of sage advice, and then it eventually transformed into *CRUSH Your Money Goals*. Initially designed as a short ten-episode run, it unexpectedly grew into a comprehensive financial education platform.

The podcast, a cornerstone of my journey, eventually expanded from just addressing debt to encompassing my five-step process covering savings, investing, and achieving financial independence without sacrificing your soul. The podcast also spilled over into real life—I began offering individual in-person and online consulting and led group meetings anywhere that asked me to—but especially to groups of people I felt I could relate to, whether that be other first-generation Americans, women, hard-working professionals, millennials, or people in debt. I soon realized that my interests covered a broad range of people and my passion lay in being a financial coach. I chose to become a financial *coach* rather than a financial *advisor* because I was frustrated with how emotional and psychological aspects that impact financial behavior are overlooked and underestimated, particularly for women and underrepresented communities. I decided to build a holistic program that would incorporate these critical human aspects into a smart money-management plan that is approachable and simple to start.

When I launched the CRUSH Your Money Goals Bootcamp in 2020, it seemed like the worst time to start a financial education business that was entirely predicated on mass gatherings. But it turned out to be a blessing in disguise because it allowed me to test my first iterations of the CRUSH model in the most trying of times—a global pandemic with high levels of uncertainty. Plus, a lot of people were looking for money guidance beyond the "set it and forget it" strategies being pushed by traditional finance experts.

The bootcamp not only worked during the pandemic, but remains applicable to every journey I've coached, manifesting uniquely for each person. Many students have found that the CRUSH steps are the gift that keeps on giving, providing a framework to rely on as they encounter major life transitions. Here's just a handful of pivotal moments where CRUSH has helped the people who use it, all of which I've had the honor of personally witnessing and guiding people through:

- Getting ready to divorce or recover from a traumatic relationship
- Empty nesting and getting ready for retirement
- Deciding whether to go for a promotion or change jobs
- Taking a leap into entrepreneurship
- Making the choice to have kids or not and how to prepare for them
- Saving up for college or other large educational investments
- Deciding what to do after a medical emergency or after a loved one has passed away
- Paying off soul-crushing debt like student loans, credit cards, and personal loans
- Getting laid off from a job with no backup plan
- Being designated as primary caregiver for an elderly parent or a disabled child
- Buying or selling a home or deciding to make major upgrades
- Finally feeling deserving of taking an extended break after a long, stressful career

CRUSH proves invaluable during these transitions, ensuring a methodical and empathetic way to manage difficult financial decisions during life's pivotal moments. Over the years, the CRUSH Bootcamp has evolved, benefiting from real-time feedback from thousands of students worldwide. This evolution is a testament to the unpredictable nature of financial journeys, and the program is stronger thanks to all of its members' contributions.

Throughout this book, I'll share with you more details about each of the CRUSH steps and habits, which can help you accelerate your progress toward financial freedom. CRUSH Your Money Goals exists to help you become a confident, badass mama jama, one hopeful habit at a time. I can't wait to go on this journey with you as your millionaire mentor. I see you, and I'm so honored that you're here.

XO,

Bernadette Joy

Introduction

I will go out on a limb and guess that you picked up this book because you are fed up with money stressing you out. Do any of these describe you right now?

- You don't have enough money saved for what matters most to you.
- You're unsure of what you should invest in.
- You feel behind in your financial status compared to people you know.
- You feel guilty for spending money even though you worked hard for it.
- Debt is eating away at your earnings and energy.
- You're wasting time on worry instead of living to your full potential.

Good news: You just picked up a gold mine with this book, and I promise you will get your bang for your buck. (Be ready for all the money puns.) Your journey with building better money habits begins with acknowledging your worth, capabilities, and self-respect.

Does it seem odd to talk about worth and self-respect in a book about financial information? The truth is, those factors are just as important as the nuts and bolts of loan terms and your 401(k). As a financial coach, I made the mistake early on of just considering math when teaching students how to pay down debt. I was surprised to learn about the variety of traumatic events students cited that influenced their money choices. They weren't mathematically sound decisions but protected them emotionally. For example, people paid for life insurance they didn't need because they saw someone else pass away without it, kept credit card debt even though they had enough cash because they grew up poor, or avoided closing certain accounts after a divorce because they reminded them of their ex.

Your past experiences are valid, and your past choices are important to reflect on, but how much longer will you let them dictate your future? My CRUSH plan will help you separate fact from fiction, prioritize your values and goals, and identify and change behaviors that could be holding you back from financial freedom. Each step of CRUSH focuses on a distinct objective:

- **C: Curate Your Accounts**—organize and simplify all your financial accounts.
- **R: Reverse Into Independence**—set tangible money goals, then work backward to identify the necessary steps to achieve them.
- **U: Understand Your (Net) Worth**—assess everything you own and owe so you have a comprehensive and objective picture of your financial health.
- **S: Spend Intentionally**—align your expenses with your financial goals, values, and beliefs.
- **H: Heal Your Money Wounds**—address and overcome the negative beliefs and patterns you have surrounding money.

Part 1 of this book will prepare you for success by helping you understand what financial freedom really looks like and rethink any money mistakes you're making. In Part 2, you'll dive into each step of the CRUSH plan in depth, learning five easy-to-understand habits per step. These habits will help you overcome both logistical challenges (finally get a handle on credit card debt) and emotional ones (having a tough conversation with your parents about how their finances might impact yours).

In each chapter of Part 2, you'll also find CRUSH Bootcamp Success Stories, where you will hear from people just like you who used these ideas to achieve their goals. Each habit also features journaling questions called Rich Reflections that encourage you to keep a money notebook while you read to reflect on triggers, fears, and negative thoughts that have been blocking your financial progress. Your brain is not good at storage; it's meant for processing. So writing your responses to these prompts will help you better remember and understand exactly why you made the choices you've made and how you can reimagine your planning approach going forward to ensure a positive financial outlook.

It *is* possible to climb out of debt, ditch the financial anxiety drama, and create financial freedom—no matter your socioeconomic status or background. That is, if you're willing to try new, smarter practices. Get ready to CRUSH Your Money Goals using the power of habits to make lasting financial changes!

PART 1

HOW TO START

WHEN YOU'RE ALREADY OVERWHELMED

Let's start off with this question:

Why aren't you rich yet?

The operative word in that question isn't "rich"; it's "yet." And there are three main solutions we'll tackle by the end of this book.

1. The first solution can be completed right now, and it takes three seconds: It's to decide. More specifically, it's deciding that you will be rich. You may have said that before, but did you really mean it? Did you commit to making it happen? In coaching, there's the simple framework that everything starts with a thought. Thoughts lead to feelings and feelings lead to actions. In order to get rich, your thoughts and feelings need to lead to rich actions.

2. The second solution is to document: A financial plan in your head isn't a plan. It's a dream, an illusion, a hope, but not a plan. A plan can be seen on paper. It is tangible. It can be understood by someone else other than you. I include Rich Reflections as an opportunity to document your plan and your progress as you build your way to wealth.

3. The third solution is simple in theory, but most people neglect it: Practice. Do things again and again. When you fail a habit, do it again. When you don't feel motivated, do it again. When it gets hard, do it again. Building smart money habits means you must commit to practicing more. I'm all for manifesting, but making, saving, and most importantly keeping money requires skill. And skills take practice. Let this book be your BFF that travels with you throughout your life and becomes a mainstay on your bookshelf or your bedside table. It will work just as well, if not better, the more you use it.

In Part 1, we're going to look at how to set yourself up for success so you can turn those thoughts into actions. You'll learn what financial freedom is and what parts of it are actually important (hint: definitely *not* complex equations and confusing economic theory). Then we'll focus on how to stop making certain mistakes that could be holding you back from getting rich.

I know what you're about to dive into will feel hard. That's because it is—*but you can do hard things*, my new financial friend! Take a deep breath and let's get to it!

Financial Literacy Is Not Enough: You Deserve Financial Independence!

"Financial literacy" refers to how much you know about the world of money and how it works...and you will learn a lot about that in this book. But my goal is not only to improve your financial literacy; it is to help you build financial independence—in other words, having enough money to live without working if you choose to. To build financial independence, you'll need a compelling vision of your money goals that isn't bogged down in complicated financial theory. How much do you *really* need to become independent? How can your finances support your lifestyle, and not the other way around? What are some ways that your financial plan can reflect your values? You're likely reading this book because you are a great learner, but now you want to level up and *do* things differently. The difference between you continuing to live paycheck to paycheck and financial independence is taking the knowledge you gain (that financial literacy) and turning it into consistent and sustainable habits.

Before we dive into smart money habits, though, I'm going to encourage you to do quite a bit of self-reflection. In this first chapter, I'll challenge the perception that achieving financial goals is too hard, time-consuming, or overwhelming. You'll learn to break self-sabotage statements, recognize that money challenges are solvable, and start viewing money as a gift, not a curse or obligation. I want you to feel empowered to prioritize your financial well-being and navigate the journey with quiet confidence (or loud, if that's more your style). Ultimately, financial independence is about embracing the power of habits and taking control of your financial destiny, and it starts with rooting out what's no longer serving you. This book isn't setting the bar at being financially literate. It's a blueprint for becoming financially free.

Understanding Financial Literacy

When you read the definition of "financial literacy," it assumes that as long as you receive the knowledge, you will be able to apply it. On the website *Investopedia*, financial literacy is summarized as:

- The ability to understand and effectively use various financial skills, including personal financial management, budgeting, and investing
- The essential foundation for a smart relationship with money

I do agree with this definition. Getting good with money is absolutely an ability and a foundation. However, I believe at some point, you must shift your focus from foundational learning to taking action. I think we can agree that just because you know something doesn't mean you'll do it! I know sugar isn't great for my diet, but I still eat donuts for breakfast! And the major concept you need to know in personal finance to be better off than most people is actually very simple: Spend less than you make and invest the difference. But actually achieving this requires consistent habits, not just knowledge.

When people refer to me as someone who teaches financial literacy, I am quick to correct them. I don't teach financial literacy; I train people for financial independence. To put it succinctly, financial literacy is learning the rules of the game of money. Financial independence is winning the game of money. I don't want you to just learn the game; I want you to be a winner!

How Financially Literate Are You?

Take out your money notebook. How would you rate yourself on financial literacy? Score yourself on a scale from 1 to 10, with 1 being completely financially illiterate and 10 being a master of all things financial.

Now, here's where the real conversation begins. What made you rate yourself the way you did? Let's dive into this together with some examples.

Marco, a business owner in my bootcamp, rated himself a 7 and explained it by saying:

> *"Well, as a small business owner, you learn through baptism by fire. I've delved into finance, read a few books, and I've got a solid base. I may not be at 10, but I'm knowledgeable."*

Another learner in my bootcamp, Loré, rated herself a 6 despite having expertise in bookkeeping for businesses as her career:

> *"I've done a lot of bookkeeping and accounting in my career, and I can really easily look at a profit and loss statement and kind of assess what's going on along with the health of a business. When it comes to my personal situation, I am not so good. I started with the exercise of figuring out my net worth, because nobody ever taught me anything. I didn't grow up with a family that even told me how to balance a checkbook. Everything I know is because of what I've learned in life. I calculated my net worth, and I'm in a better spot than I would have guessed I was, and that I think is all from just the hard work that I've done in life."*

Then there's Karla, who rated herself a 4 at the start of my bootcamp, since she was feeling a bit overwhelmed despite having read several books:

> *"Yeah, people talk to me about financial stuff, and I listen, but it's hard to comprehend. I'm here to learn, though. I think courses will help me."*

Do you resonate with Marco, Loré, or Karla? You've been trying your hardest, but you just can't seem to get to that 10 you think you need to be when it comes to financial literacy?

Now, here's a bold statement: Anyone who reads this book can become a 10 in financial literacy. Surprising, right? Let me clarify. The fallacy that people have is that they believe they must learn *everything* about money to be a 10: The stock market. Taxes. Interest rates. Inflation. Real estate. Passive income. But the truth is that money is a wide-ranging subject, and it would be impossible to learn all of it at an expert level.

Instead, reframe your approach to financial literacy and aim to become a 10 by learning the pieces that are most relevant to you, your personal situation, and the way you want to align your values to your money. If you filter out all the noise that isn't relevant to you, your lifestyle, and the way that you want to manage your finances, it is actually not very complicated to become a 10.

For instance, as a small business owner, Marco doesn't need to delve into topics that are better suited for corporate professionals working for a large company. Similarly, you do not have to understand the entire tax code to be financially independent; that is what tax experts are for. I'll teach you the foundation—the essentials that you really need for financial success.

The key is to focus on what matters to you and become a 10 in those aspects. If you are someone who worries about not understanding the stock market, but you don't plan to invest in it, relax. If that's not your interest, there are numerous other ways to build wealth and invest. Most of my wealth has not been built through the stock market. It has been built through real estate and being an entrepreneur. And I excelled at them because I rejected the idea that the stock market is the only way to invest.

So, let's embark on this journey together. Commit to becoming a 10 in the financial literacy nuggets that will truly make a difference in your financial life. Are you ready to unveil your financial power? Let's do this!

Question What You've Heard Before about Money

I don't believe that there are any "beginners" in personal finance. You have actually been practicing personal finance for a very long time, from the first coin you put in your piggy bank as a child. You are not a beginner when it comes to money, even if you feel like it right now. Chances are, someone else made you feel that way.

Let's revisit what our friend Karla said: "People talk to me about financial stuff, and I listen, but it's hard to comprehend." Have you tried to learn financial concepts before, but the info just doesn't stick?

The good news is that I don't believe it's your fault (or any of our faults). As I looked for my own sources of financial knowledge, I learned that so much of what is labeled as "financial literacy" is flawed in not only how it is taught but what is taught—and *who* is teaching it. Despite the fact that I have bachelor's and master's degrees in business, my third degree in psychology has been the most useful in building money habits. Understanding behavior matters more than understanding math.

For example, a real estate agent will always tell you it's a great time to buy a home. A credit card company will bombard you with pop-up ads about its travel rewards and points programs but conveniently bury the 27% interest in the fine print. Financial advisors throw around complex phrases like "basis points," "tax advantaged," and "dollar cost averaging," and suddenly you feel like you cannot do it on your own. And do not get me started on life insurance agents who sell life insurance as an investment!

A leader in my CRUSH Bootcamp once told me she heard it was a bad idea to pay off her student loans. My first question after someone tells me what they heard is: "Who told you that?" It turned out to be the used-car salesman (no, not a metaphor, an actual used-car salesman) who was telling her it was completely okay to finance her entire car loan and not worry about her student loans. When she responded out loud, she realized how silly it had been of her to listen to the salesman's advice while he was trying to make a sale. Many of us have been sold bad money advice without even realizing it.

I acknowledge that some professionals are genuinely trying to educate customers, but the conflict of interest in many programs can misguide learners. Personal finance education for high schoolers, now mandated in many states, seems like a great progression since I left high school in the early 2000s. But when I researched more closely, I learned that banks often sponsor these courses to capture young students and promote their financial products, disguising them as free education for their local communities.

It's essential to question the source and motivation behind financial advice you hear. If you've felt confused like Karla, it's because what was communicated to you added complexity. It was geared to make you feel confused to maximize the benefit of the advice giver.

My Journey from $300K of Debt to Financial Independence

Until my thirties, I had never personally met someone who successfully retired with enough money, let alone retired early because they were financially independent. My father was forced into retirement in his seventies after the advertising company he'd dedicated decades of his life to let him go and save his salary to increase their bottom line.

You could say that my mom retired early, as she stopped working as a bookkeeper in her fifties, but only after she had several health conditions that kept her out of work until her medical leave ran out. She found herself unable to keep up with basic computer skills she hadn't needed when she'd entered the workforce decades before.

I later found out that my parents hid the fact they were struggling in retirement, and my mother decided to clean houses to close the gap. Eventually, my parents decided to sell my childhood home in Queens, New York, and move to Las Vegas to stretch their social security checks and the small nest egg they'd built over the years. Many of my money fears are rooted in watching my parents' tumultuous retirement journey.

On the other side of the spectrum, I met wealthier people, particularly as I started my career in financial services and technology startups, who thrived on the mentality that sleep was for the dead. Growing up in New York City, I felt incredibly pressured to show how much I was working and prove I was somebody important. After I burned out and decided to get a master's degree in business, I found myself surrounded by workaholics as classmates.

It was that same MBA program that precipitated my interest, or rather panic, in personal finance. My last semester of classes kicked off in January, and I was scheduled to graduate in April. It dawned on me that I had not once looked at the amount of student loans I had borrowed, but I surmised the amount would be manageable since I had been making payments along the way, as I was working a part-time job while going to school full-time.

So, you can imagine my shock when I finally logged in and found out I had over $72,000 in student loans and that they were accruing interest daily that would equate to a Venti mocha latte at Starbucks every day. I had no job prospects and no idea how I was going to pay back what I owed. That shock quickly turned into a deep shame spiral—I found myself sobbing on the floor of my home office, berating myself for making such an expensive mistake. Financial independence was not even on my radar. I felt financially stupid.

I was able to turn things around, though: I paid off all $72,000 of student loans in less than a year and subsequently paid off the remainder of my $300,000 in total debt in three years, including my mortgage. I was debt-free by age thirty-four, thanks to the habits I will teach you in this book. Even if you have no intention of retiring early, I encourage you to explore how financial independence can give you a wider range of choices for your life. Even if you have to keep working, or choose to, you can look forward to pushing rest, rejuvenation, and hobbies higher up on your priority list.

Balancing the Two Sides of Financial Independence: Net Worth and Self-Worth

As I paid off my debt and eventually became a millionaire, I learned that there are two sides to financial independence, which must be consciously balanced and rebalanced in order for you to feel true freedom: net worth and self-worth.

Net Worth

On one side of financial independence is the mathematical measure known as net worth. Simply put, net worth is everything you own minus everything you owe. The difference is your net worth.

We will discuss the specific details of how to determine your net worth in later chapters. What you need to start training yourself to do is to calculate, track, and make decisions based on this number. Since the vast majority of people making financial decisions rarely track this number accurately, they make financial decisions based off of generalities rather than the specifics of their unique situation. It's like asking a doctor to give you a medical diagnosis without examining you or knowing the results of various blood tests. You must know your numbers accurately to make good financial choices.

Self-Worth

On the other side of financial freedom is the worth that most financial experts ignore, but that I argue is more important to measure: self-worth. That's the mental peace you get from knowing that you are making the best financial decisions for yourself. My therapist once told me that I had a lot of self-esteem but very little self-worth. I had no idea they were different concepts back then, but becoming financially independent helped me understand the difference. Self-esteem is more reliant on external factors like awards, achievements, and what people think of you. Self-worth is internal. It's intuitively trusting that you are good enough and worthy of being loved. I think of self-esteem as loud confidence and self-worth as quiet confidence. I learned that financial freedom doesn't need to be loud and flashy. Financial freedom is knowing you are good enough even if no one has any clue how rich or poor you are.

Have you ever met a wealthy person who clearly lacked self-worth? It usually shows up in the form of bragging about how much money they have, judging others for what they have, or just giving you the icks when you hear them speak about themselves or other people. I have met several wealthy people who are sad, if not depressed, or are constantly striving for more money in the hopes that they will finally feel loved. They have high self-esteem but low self-worth. I can identify it easily now, because I used to be the same.

The truth is you cannot achieve real financial independence without self-worth, even if you have a billion dollars in the bank. In fact, the beauty of self-worth is that it's not connected to how much money you have right now. You can start growing self-worth without money—you just need a lot of intentionality in cultivating three important beliefs:

1. **You must believe you are worthy of wealth.** I firmly believe that money doesn't change people. Instead, it's like a karaoke mic—it simply amplifies the voice you've had all along. The tone and content of what you sing is entirely up to you. You must believe that you deserve not to worry about money every day, and that you can and should be able to afford the experiences and possessions that matter to you. Craving financial independence isn't a crime. It isn't selfish. It is something you are allowed to say you deserve.

2. **You must believe that you are capable.** Are you terrible at math? That's okay; the most math you'll need is fourth-grade level. If you can do addition, subtraction, multiplication, and division (you can even use a calculator!), you'll be just fine. If you keep saying that you can't or that it's not possible, it will inevitably become a self-fulfilling prophecy.

3. **You must respect yourself.** This is the most overlooked part of growing your self-worth. You need to respect yourself so much that you will stop breaking promises to yourself. Would you break a promise to someone who you respect? No? Then start behaving like someone who others don't want to disappoint. Respect yourself not only today but respect your future self. When you say you are going to do something, actually do it.
   - You say you'll save more money? *Do it.*
   - You say you'll pay off your debt? *Finish it.*
   - You say you deserve a vacation? *Pay for it in cash, in advance, and come home to no more credit card bills, because you deserve to come back stress-free.*

Whenever I am faced with an obstacle or really rough day, I remind myself that it's an opportunity to prove that I meant it when I said I would achieve financial freedom, no matter what.

You are worthy. You are capable. You will respect yourself. Why? Because you will grow your net worth and self-worth. Because you deserve financial independence. Say it loud for the people in the back to hear!

Turn Self-Sabotage Into Self-Empowerment

When most of us start thinking about financial independence, our brains start spiraling down a negative path and announcing dire statements like: *I'll never get there. I won't ever be able to retire at this rate. People like me never have enough money to stop working.* I learned from coaching hundreds of people that the biggest block to many people's financial progress is negative thoughts like these—or what I refer to as self-sabotage statements.

Self-sabotage statements are things you say to yourself that ultimately stop you from moving toward independence and instead encourage you to settle for what's essentially financial chaos. I call them *self*-sabotage because they are rarely things other people are saying to you directly—though they are often reflective of statements you've heard from friends, family, and society at large that made you believe they were true.

In this section, I'll review some common self-sabotage statements I hear from my CRUSH members and offer you alternative Millionaire Move actions to take. Practicing these more positive, empowering options will help you build the resilience you need to achieve your financial goals. I call them Millionaire Moves because they inspire *action*. They energize and encourage you to keep moving, even when you're not ready. Even if they feel silly or untrue right now, actually say them out loud as you read through them.

SELF-SABOTAGE STATEMENT	MILLIONAIRE MOVE
This is too hard for me.	**Do hard things.**

If pursuing financial independence feels hard, it's because it is, in fact, hard. But that doesn't mean it's impossible. Whenever you find a habit challenging, remind yourself that you are capable of overcoming difficulties. You've done hard things before, and you didn't die. This is not the first hard challenge you've faced, and this will not be the last. Financially independent people don't give up just because it's hard. They double down and find a way to take action and achieve their goals.

SELF-SABOTAGE STATEMENT	MILLIONAIRE MOVE
I don't have time for this.	Find time to make money one of your top three priorities.

I get it; you're busy. You've got this, that, and all the other things as valid reasons that your money goals have been put on the back burner. That's the old self-sabotaging mentality, though. It's time to prioritize your financial well-being by dedicating time to managing your money, regardless of your busy schedule. You have the same number of hours in a day as every other human on earth. The difference is that those who become financially independent make time for their money goals. So, take action: Pull your calendar out now and find at least one hour a week to spend prioritizing your financial independence.

SELF-SABOTAGE STATEMENT	MILLIONAIRE MOVE
I am overwhelmed.	Take a deep breath and figure this out. This is not life or death. You can solve this.

I hear this self-sabotage statement a lot from my CRUSH Bootcamp, and I get it. As you read this book, you might also feel overwhelmed at certain points. You will read some of the harder habits and think, *This woman is bananas*, and you'll want to close the book and stop. Financially independent achievers keep moving despite feeling overwhelmed—but that does not mean that you ignore your feelings altogether. At any moment that you feel overwhelmed, commit to pausing and taking a deep breath. Literally. Put the book down and take a deep breath. Drink some water and take a walk around the block. Then when you calm down and recenter yourself, get back to it.

SELF-SABOTAGE STATEMENT	MILLIONAIRE MOVE
I don't want to deal with my money.	Get excited about having more money!

As a kid, I would get so excited when I got those thin, rectangular envelopes on my birthday or Christmas because I knew there was money inside. (Heck, as an adult I'm still excited to be gifted twenty bucks from a relative!) Try to recapture those childhood vibes so that even small amounts of money excite you! Do you think of your money as a burden—something to deal with, to bear, that feels heavy and obligatory? Or do you view money as an honor? Like, wow, what an honor to have this money I worked so hard for! I earned this, and now I get to put this gift toward whatever it is that I want! Shift your language to treating your finances as something to be psyched about, not a task to dread. Remind yourself that money is a gift—a valuable resource and a reward for your efforts.

SELF-SABOTAGE STATEMENT	MILLIONAIRE MOVE
They are not on board.	Make this journey your own. The people who are meant to be on this journey with you will rise to the occasion.

Most of us have other people influencing our finances in one way or another. For example, one of the most common questions I get from women is, "How do I get my partner on board with my financial goals?" Or maybe your family isn't good with money, and your parents need you to help them in retirement. Maybe your friends keep inviting you to expensive brunches (seriously, why are we paying $20 for scrambled eggs on toast?!). Maybe all your coworkers do is moan and groan about how they are underpaid.

Even if you are in a committed relationship, come from a tough childhood, or are surrounded by naysayers, remember that your financial journey is unique, and those who align with your goals are welcome to join you on the path to success. My husband's journey is separate from my own, even though there are absolutely overlaps. Years ago when I decided I was going to be rich, I told him it was up to him if he wanted to come along for the ride.

I find "My journey is my own" especially hard for my fellow first-generation friends to swallow because they culturally feel guilty for leaving loved ones behind in pursuit of their own financial stability. I'm not suggesting that you hate on people who don't want to go on the journey with you. If they don't want to or can't come right now, that is okay—even if it is someone you love dearly. They're on one path and you're on another. Sometimes they will cross, and sometimes they will be far apart. It doesn't mean either of your paths is wrong. Just don't let their reluctance or doubts hold *you* back.

That said, you may be pleasantly surprised by who will watch you and who will join you. I know this because I've had hundreds of strangers join me on my journey to financial freedom, who found me on social media, read one of my articles, or watched one of my videos. I also know this because my family used to make fun of me and my husband for being cheap...but when we paid off my student loans, they suddenly followed suit, and now all of us are free of student loans.

Instead of waiting for others to get on board, choo choo your own train and see who comes along when the time is right for them.

SELF-SABOTAGE STATEMENT	MILLIONAIRE MOVE
I'm too young; or I'm too old.	**Prepare like your best years are yet to come.**

Young people who join me tend to have the YOLO (you only live once) mentality and want to spend their money and deal with saving later. On the flip side, I have learners in their fifties or older who regret not starting sooner.

In my current cohort of CRUSH Bootcamp, the youngest member is twenty and the oldest is seventy-two. I've had the honor of meeting a wonderful woman named Deb who lives in New York City and turned age seventy-two the year I am writing this book. No matter your age, you will likely need money in the future. It's less about how old you are; it's more about how committed you choose to be with the time you have going forward. It's impossible to start too young. Many of the habits we'll discuss in this book are ones that you can share even with the children in your life to help them start early.

But even if you feel like you're on the "older" side of life, I'd like for you to believe, as I do, that your future is worth protecting. So why not make the most of those years by giving financial freedom a shot?

Since you're reading this, I already know your best years aren't behind you. In fact, regardless of your age, consider your best years are ahead of you. At the time I write this book, I am thirty-nine years old, and I'm looking forward to entering my forties. Not only do I think my best years are ahead, but I'm not even anywhere close to my prime!

As we close out this chapter, I encourage you to borrow at least one of these Millionaire Moves, or to write down three of your own on sticky notes and post them where you can see them regularly. Building smart money habits requires *doing*, not just saying. Congrats on your first Millionaire Move: finishing this first chapter! Keep going!

RICH REFLECTIONS

On a scale from 1 to 10, how far-fetched does that financial independence number feel to you?

What self-sabotage statements have you said recently that are making it feel further away?

What's one Millionaire Move you can commit to making? You can use one of mine or write your own on a sticky note where you can see it every day.

CHAPTER 2

Stop Losing Money Making These Five Mistakes

I have a bad habit that I'm embarrassed to share with you. In the past, I did not brush my teeth very thoroughly. Yes, as an adult. I know, gross. For me, brushing my teeth felt more like pulling my teeth. Of course, I did it every day, twice a day. But I never looked forward to it and tried to rush through it as fast as possible. This mistake has unfortunately cost me a bunch of money—literally tens of thousands of dollars in oral surgeries, crowns, fillings, and braces and retainers that never really did their full job. And my smile is something I'll never be fully confident about.

Three years ago, I finally resolved to learn proper dental hygiene. I felt silly but I asked my dentist to show me how to properly brush and floss my teeth as an adult. She sat there patiently with that giant set of teeth and a giant toothbrush to show me how, the same way she taught children to do it.

The point in sharing this embarrassing secret is that before we can build smart money habits, we must address the mistakes we're making first. It won't be easy, and it might even be a little embarrassing. Every person I've ever coached personally has had a money mistake that felt shameful to them, so don't worry. There's nothing wrong with you. Being ashamed to admit you have a bad habit isn't a good reason to keep doing it. This chapter will outline five money mistakes you may not even realize you're making, and you'll learn how to replace them with smarter habits we'll discuss in Part 2.

MONEY MISTAKE #1:

Juggling Too Many Money Goals At Once

This is the most common bad habit I encounter with financial-coaching clients—trying to tackle a bunch of financial goals at the same time. Juggling too many goals is a recipe for feeling overwhelmed and slowing down your overall financial progress. I've had more than one person ask me something like, "How do I save money, pay off my credit card debt, save for a house, and make sure my kids go to college?" Sound familiar? That sounds overwhelming because it *is*, and I'm here to tell you that most times, less is better.

Despite being told that multitasking is the key to success, humans are best suited to accomplish goals as "monotaskers." In fact, a 2010 *Psychonomic Bulletin & Review* study found that just 2.5% of people can multitask effectively. This means that your brain can only focus on one task at a time, as neuropsychologist Cynthia Kubu explained in a 2021 interview with the Cleveland Clinic. In reality, you're not actually multitasking—instead, you are switching between multiple tasks in really rapid succession. And if you're doing a bunch of tasks and switching between them constantly, you're more prone to making mistakes, overlooking important details, and slowing down your overall progress.

I have not completely kicked the multitasking habits I was raised to believe would make me successful: I still try to watch video podcasts while folding laundry. And if you are talking to me while my phone is in my hand, I am certainly fighting the urge to scroll through social media. However, I can confirm that slowing down and reducing the number of financial tasks I manage on a daily and monthly basis has absolutely been a game changer in making me a millionaire.

So, if you catch yourself thinking, *I need to save money, pay off debt, send my kids to college, and buy a new car*, hit the brakes. Put them in order by priority, one at a time. When I started, my sole focus was paying down my student loans. I knocked them out in nine months because that was my laser-sharp focus. Now I never have to worry about paying student loans again. Rather than think of all your money goals as separate entities, think of them as milestones that need to be in priority order.

Marie Kondo your money goals—declutter, rearrange, and restack them so you can keep your eyes on that one goal: financial independence. Finish one milestone, then move on to the next. Not only will you get there faster, but you will also enjoy yourself along the way.

WHO IS STRESSED ABOUT MONEY?

In 2022, the American Psychological Association reported that 65% of adults cited money as a source of stress, the highest level recorded since 2015. A closer look at demographic differences showed that 75% of Latino and 67% of Black adults reported money as a source of stress (a higher percentage than white and Asian adults), with the economy and housing costs being top of mind.

MONEY MISTAKE #2:
Comparing to the Wrong Success Stories

The second most common mistake I've witnessed as a money coach is comparing yourself to others in ways that aren't meaningful. They say comparison is the thief of joy, but I think of comparison more like that petty friend from high school who always spills the juicy gossip. It feels fun in the moment, but then you feel icky afterward. Comparison really does nothing for you in the long run, even if it's fun for a little while.

Especially in the US, we often compare ourselves to ridiculously wealthy people, like billionaires. Now, you don't have to be a billionaire to be financially independent and successful. Honestly, being a billionaire is overkill in my opinion—I don't believe any human needs to spend that much money in a lifetime! When I realized that one billionaire equals one thousand millionaires or one thousand Bernadettes, it completely blew my mind.

I've met millionaires who downplay it, saying they're not rich. I have even gotten comments online saying, "A million dollars isn't even that much nowadays." Come on, if you're a millionaire, you're rich. In fact, the number of people with total wealth over $1 million remains relatively small in size, around 59.4 million, or 1.1% of all adults worldwide. And here's what I've found in common across many rich people: They build assets that generate income for them so they can work less. Yet instead of comparing assets like retirement accounts, skills, and professional networks, we compare ourselves to those who we think are richer than us because of the cars they drive, the houses they flaunt, the vacations they post on social media, and the perceived success they have in their careers.

Interestingly, according to the Federal Reserve, from 2019 to 2022, the average household net worth in the US went up by 23% to over a million dollars, despite a worldwide pandemic. Becoming a millionaire puts you in the top 10% in the US and the top 1% globally…and it gives you the freedom to focus on things that truly matter to you without stressing about basic expenses.

FIND AN ADVISOR WHO GETS YOU

My experience with traditional financial advisors (72.1% of whom are white) was difficult as an Asian American woman. Discussing finances with someone who did not know me personally felt invasive and uncomfortable, especially when they assumed that their money experience was similar to mine. My last financial advisor was only interested in speaking about investments, when my biggest money stressor was paying my student loans and mortgages. He did not understand that I had grown up with a deep emphasis on education and was carrying shame, inherited from my Filipino immigrant parents, around my debt. Look for mentors who will take the time to get to know you as a whole person.

The median net worth increased to $192,900 for a household. (I told you we only need fourth-grade math! The median is the middle value in a range, which is different than the average.) Yep, that's a big difference. The thing is, when we talk about averages, those ultra-wealthy folks skew them.

The $192,900 median net worth should catch your eye—as you will learn from calculating your financial independence number, that's not going to cut it for true financial freedom. Yet that's where a lot of people currently sit. Most of us don't compare ourselves using that number, though—we instead make comparisons where we look "bad."

Financial independence, to me, is about building a life that feels free on the inside, not just looking flashy on the outside. That's why comparisons tend to fall short—they don't take into consideration what's going on behind the scenes (like in your retirement account). The point is this: You don't actually know who's rich and who's not based on what you see externally. So, there's no point in comparing what you have to someone else's perceived wealth. It's not what you think it is based on their material possessions.

So, my advice? Stop comparing yourself to billionaires, and don't compare yourself to most people, either—because most people unfortunately won't have enough money saved to retire comfortably. My CRUSH Bootcamp are not regular people. They prove this by getting up early on Sunday mornings to take personal finance classes with me, when it would be easier to sleep in. Likely, you are not like most people either—you've picked up this book and are making Millionaire Moves.

Instead of comparing to external success stories, honor that your financial independence milestones are unique to you. It's not about what others have; it's about what you need. Establish your milestones based on your own values and aspirations, not what would get the most likes on your social media feed.

I want you to think about what financial freedom looks like for you by writing down your responses to the following questions. Even better, draw a picture or create a vision board to show what you want.

- Who's there with you? Think beyond just your immediate family and friends.
- What are you doing? What are you doing that you've always wanted to do?
- When is it happening? How soon do you want this to happen?
- Most importantly, why are you doing it? Is this life unique to you, or are you copying someone else's vision?

I'll be real with you—in 2023, I was burned out. I had amazing opportunities to build my business and grow my platform and was happy with my milestones. That is, until I compared myself to other personal finance experts who were getting paid more, getting booked more, and getting more likes on social media. Hoping to "catch up," I frantically tried to do more than everyone else so I could come out on top. If they wrote five articles for *Forbes*, I wrote twenty. If they got five hundred likes on Instagram, I agonized over how I could make the algorithm love me. If they got paid $5,000, I thought, *Let me see how I can get $10,000!*

I spread myself so thin that I hit a breaking point, and I suddenly felt very lost. The reason I became a financial coach was to help other women like me achieve authentic freedom. When did it turn into a competition? I felt so embarrassed. It led me to quiet my voice. Then when people said hurtful things to me, I was too exhausted to fight back.

Once I realized how I'd turned freedom into a competition, I stopped the comparison trap and went back to my roots—helping people most overlooked by traditional financial services and educating them, rather than selling to them. I started to say things I had not heard other people say. Surprisingly, the habit of comparing myself to my own definition of success rather than to others' definitions gave me the opportunity to author this book.

Commit today to stop falling into the comparison trap by instead focusing on your unique values and building a life that feels free on the inside. Financial independence is even more within reach when it's about what matters to you, not what others think. In a later chapter, I'll share how you can find the right people to compare to in a healthy way, and even get them to be your millionaire mentors.

MONEY MISTAKE #3:
Giving Out Discounts Nobody Asked For

All right, let's delve into the third mistake—something I've spoken about a hundred times and a topic I call out in my live talks: giving out discounts nobody asked for. It's time to put an end to this habit that is literally costing you thousands. I'm saying it for me, and I'm saying it for all of us. This has always been a tough one for me to practice myself as a first-generation Filipino American. (Filipinos love asking for discounts—it's basically our love language.) There are several ways that these discounts can show up in your life, from accepting less pay to thinking of burnout as a badge of honor. Let's look at each in more detail.

Undercharging or Accepting Less Pay

According to the Pew Research Center, the gender pay gap has remained about the same in the United States over the past twenty years or so. In 2022, women earned an average of 82% of what men earned, similar to where the pay gap stood in 2002, when women earned 80% as much as men. Of course, there are larger economic and societal forces at play here. Although you can't control other people, you can control what you are willing to ask for or do.

So, what are these discounts we're talking about? Well, the obvious one is undercharging. We all know that one, right? In the coaching field, I personally know a lot of coaches who undercharge because they'd rather have a full client roster than a committed one. Undercharging also looks like being afraid to negotiate for pay or sticking to your guns and saying, "My price is my price" when someone asks to pay you less. It's often caused by impostor syndrome or maybe it's the fear of losing clients. But here's the reality check—if you undervalue your time, others will too. Conversely, if you stop giving out discounts nobody asked for, eventually people will stop asking for them!

Overdelivering

Undercharging can also look like giving away extra time or effort—in other words, working too hard or always going above and beyond. Overdelivering is a form of discount that is certainly costing you thousands. There's a thin line between going the extra mile and running a marathon. Why are you going above and beyond what you're getting paid for? It's a question worth pondering. When I worked at a big bank, I was so used to the narrative that you work for the job you want instead of the job you have. Then I found myself doing my boss's job for half of her pay.

Finding that sweet spot where you deliver exceptional work and value without compromising your well-being takes practice. The warning sign that you're giving out too many discounts is when you start feeling resentful. It's a path I hope I can prevent you from going down. I learned the hard way that it takes a very long time to get back to a path of gratitude once you've gone down the resentment spiral.

Saying Yes Too Often

Another way discounts manifest in your time and money is saying yes when you really want to say no. We've all been there. The fear of missing out or the desire to please others can lead us to agree to things we should decline.

This one I'm proud to say I've really begun to grasp in the last few years. For example, I recently turned down a speaking gig because, even though it was an opportunity to stand on a stage in front of two hundred people, the organizer offered *no* pay despite requesting to use my name, image, copyrighted content, and network to promote her event. For a Sunday morning event at that! The "reward" she offered was that I could promote my business, but I did not need that—I already have amazing clients.

Discounting Your Time with Trivial Tasks

Here's a discount I know most women are offering without realizing it—doing tasks below our pay grade. Some of us are still stuck believing that we can save money by doing tasks that can be easily outsourced. I coach many entrepreneurs who clean the house, handle mundane tasks, and act more like assistants than bosses even when their businesses can afford to pay others. If that sounds like you, outsource that stuff so you can focus on what truly matters. Outsourcing is not a sign of weakness; it's a smart move to optimize your time and energy.

Accepting Burnout

The grand finale of this discount fiesta—accepting burnout as a badge of honor—is a toxic mentality that many of us have fallen victim to. I think of burnout as me discounting the value of my life. I know that sounds dramatic, but it wasn't until I decided that my life was worth more than I gave it credit for that I stopped accepting burnout as an acceptable and constant state of being. I realized that the times that I felt most burned out were when I gave away my precious time and limited energy to things that didn't mean that much to me. Burnout is not a symbol of success; it's a sign that boundaries need to be drawn. I stopped thinking of boundaries like a wall or a fence and more like the red velvet rope to the VIP section. In later chapters, we'll chat about who gets let in and who you'll have to nicely turn away.

So, stop giving out discounts on your time, energy, and mental well-being, my friend! Your net worth and self-worth will grow by leaps and bounds if you value your life accordingly.

MONEY MISTAKE #4:
Accepting Debt As a Long-Term Lifestyle

Here's the fourth bad money habit that needs to hit the road—accepting debt as a long-term lifestyle rather than a short-term solution. Yep, even that mortgage and those student loans should not be sticking around for-ever. It's time for a shift in perspective, especially in the US, where we've somehow bought into the idea that major life milestones, like buying a house, getting married, or going to school, can only happen with a side of debt.

Believe it or not, financing a big purchase is *not* the only option. We've been conditioned to believe that a car purchase requires a car loan and emergencies demand a credit card. That's total crap. Relying on debt to get you through challenging times doesn't need to be your default habit. Pay-ing for big purchases outright will absolutely change the way you manage money forever. Once I decided that debt wasn't going to be my long-term lifestyle, I had more confidence in my money decisions and was able to build better habits.

Now, I'm not saying having debt right now is the end of the world. If you need it in the short term, that's understandable. If you come from a family that has no financial means, a student loan may be necessary. If you are in a critical medical emergency, you're not going to turn away the ambulance because of the potential bill. What's crucial is acknowledging that debt is a short-term solution, not a permanent companion on your financial journey. There needs to be a clear deadline for paying off that debt—and it probably shouldn't be the one the financer gives you. The longer you hold on to the debt, the more passive income they make from you.

The average debt scenario in the US is staggering—no wonder people feel overwhelmed. In the middle of 2023, US households were swimming in the highest amount of debt in history, sitting at a mind-blowing $17.3 trillion, according to the Federal Reserve Bank of New York. And just to give you a visual, that's $17,300,000,000,000. To make things worse, in 2023, the average credit card interest rate according to *Forbes* was a whopping 27.81%. I think that's absolutely criminal. I can't even fathom how that's allowed. But let's not get too bogged down by the numbers. Ask yourself: Why are you relying on debt to achieve your dreams instead of relying on your own ability first? Keep repeating this—*I am capable of hard things!*

One of my favorite early financial-coaching clients, named Angela, was a star student. She was witty, she was sharp, and she was gung ho on getting her debt paid down, moving toward early retirement, and saving up for her daughter's college fund. However, she was always relying on credit cards anytime an unexpected expense came up.

But she began following the CRUSH plan to a T and built up her emergency fund to several thousand dollars. She had never intentionally saved money like that in the past. I was proud of her, and she was proud of herself. While she was still in my program, the unexpected knocked on her door in the form of complete flooding of her basement. I mean, a wading-in-water, belongings-completely-soaked kind of flood.

She, however, stayed calm and collected…but then did exactly as her longtime habits trained her to do and charged the repairs on her credit card. The next time we met, and I reviewed her accounts, I saw the thousands of dollars on her credit card and asked her what happened.

Again, coolly and calmly, she explained the situation and said it needed to be fixed. When I asked her why she charged it on her credit card instead of using the cash in her emergency fund, she fell silent.

She simply hadn't thought of it. She was so used to charging emergency expenses to her credit card, it had become a habit, even though she now had the cash to cover it. She admitted feeling silly, but I assured her there was nothing to feel silly about. You might relate to this, even going all the way back to your childhood if you grew up in a household that didn't have much cash savings to rely on.

Don't be too hard on yourself if you're trying to overcome debt mistakes. What's more important is practicing a better choice moving forward. Debt keeps you living in the past. In fact, any debt you're holding on to is essentially anchoring you to previous financial decisions. Starting now, think of debt as a last resort, not the first option you turn to when a financial challenge comes your way. In Part 2, I'll teach you how to start paying off your debt faster and use credit cards as a tool for moving toward your financial freedom, not further away from it.

MONEY MISTAKE #5:
Choosing Fear over Freedom in Making Money Choices

If you find yourself hesitating and second-guessing financial choices, fear is probably dictating how you manage your money. This mistake makes frequent appearances in one-on-one sessions with my financial-coaching clients, and it's time to tackle it head-on.

You may have heard of the famous fear responses in psychology—the common trio is fight, flight, or freeze. These date back to when humans had to worry about things like bear attacks and quickly had to choose whether to punch the bear, run away from the bear, or play dead and hope the bear moseyed along, past them and their clan.

Thankfully, most of us don't have to worry about animal attacks or hunting for our next meal on a daily basis. Instead, we've transferred our fear responses to the modern world's everyday threats, like bosses who suck or losing our income. However, in training people to achieve financial independence, I encounter two additional fear responses that are quite common and sometimes occur in combination with the first three:

1. **The fourth fear response, which is lesser known, is fawn.** Fawning is a trauma response where you use people-pleasing behavior to avoid conflict. It often looks like a client telling me how wonderful I am and how much they're learning while secretly avoiding the work they promised to finish. They want to look like model students more than they want to be model money managers for themselves. It doesn't mean they're bad people. It's likely how they've been able to survive attacks from aggressors in the past.

2. **The fifth fear response is what I call the financial freak-out.** It's when someone enters a period of irrational money behavior or an emotional spiral after being hit with a financial challenge. This might look like going on a shopping spree after hearing unwelcome news, accepting low-paying work out of desperation, or pulling out money from investments even though they know it will incur a penalty. I've learned that it's often a response made to reassert control when they suddenly feel out of control of their situation.

   It's okay if you've employed this fear response in the past. In future chapters, you will learn some habits that can help you minimize these financial freak-outs, if not avoid them altogether. The first step is recognizing that this behavior is a response to fear, not an indication that you are a bad person or that you're dumb with money.

Since there aren't many bear attacks nowadays, what are we *really* afraid of? There are some obvious things, like the fear of going homeless or hungry, the fear of losing your job or business, or the fear of a major medical emergency that could bankrupt you. In the context of pursing financial independence, I've seen these types of fears bubble up to the surface and stop people from reaching their greatest potential.

Let's confront some of the common fears I see from my clients so you can recognize if they appear in your own life. They probably aren't new to you, but I want you to think about how they've influenced how you move your money.

Fear of Judgment from Family and Friends

Even my most outspoken clients, who claim they don't care what people think, still make choices based on what people may or may not say about them. This can manifest in the form of buying things to fit in, spending more than you need to impress others, or posting only the highlights to your social media in the hopes that others will notice you. Fear of judgment can also manifest in not pursuing passions because your family might not approve, or in staying in a job you hate because the corporate title is good. For example, even though I knew in my early twenties that corporate life wasn't for me, I didn't immediately quit because I was fearful of what my family would say if I were to leave for something unconventional.

Personally, I stopped telling my parents about things that excited me, like travel or healthy food or exploring new hobbies. As immigrants from the Philippines, they considered those things luxuries that were a waste of money. I only recently started to genuinely enjoy those little luxuries, once I started learning that money is replenishable, even if you've made mistakes in the past.

This fear of judgment is rooted in ancient human behaviors and needs—namely, being part of a tribe and having a sense of belonging. It's one of the most basic human needs to have others like us. What's become even more challenging is that in the age of social media, our circle of approval can sometimes extend even to strangers on the Internet.

When I'm in a situation where I'm fearing judgment, here are two things I constantly remind myself:

1. Everyone is mostly worried about themselves; they're not paying as much attention to you as you think.
2. The most important person that should be proud of you…is you! As long as you love yourself and the person you're becoming, who cares what they think?

Fear of Losing Money

Humans are wired to avoid pain even more than we are wired to pursue gains. Many CRUSH Bootcamp members will avoid making even minimal-risk financial decisions because of past experiences in which they lost money. This is especially true related to investment decisions that went wrong. The challenge with facing this fear is that it often dates to one's experiences growing up, perhaps in which the family narrative was that money was rare rather than available, or that money should be protected and saved at all costs.

A brave example in my CRUSH Bootcamp is Monica, who became so great at stashing cash that she had way more than she needed in savings, but she was afraid to invest because of family trauma she'd experienced in the past. She felt the need to have a surplus of cash, always waiting for the shoe to drop.

But after working through our bootcamp, she finally decided to give a shot at putting the maximum amount she could into her employer retirement fund. She resolved she would try it for a paycheck or two, putting much more into her investments, and see how she felt. If it felt too emotionally taxing, she would roll it back. I was so proud of her for giving it that shot because it showed that she started seeing money as renewable rather than scarce.

Fear of Failure

This is an obvious one. No one likes to feel like a loser. It's natural to have anxiety about trying new skills if you don't think you'll succeed. However, an interesting phenomenon I've witnessed, particularly in my female learners, is having such a strong fear of failure that you're not even willing to give new things a try.

I recently taught an investing class in which I showed a list of potential index funds with some basic information: their ticker symbols, their expense ratios, their return percentages, and their descriptions. I then asked the class to each choose which investment they would personally pick from the list. No one responded immediately. I then told the class there was no wrong answer; it was a matter of personal preference. We weren't investing any real money after all. Slowly, one by one, students raised their hands and explained why they chose what they chose, and all their responses were totally logical. Part of the fear of failure when it comes to money is the false assumption that there is only one right way to wealth.

Interestingly, one student didn't respond at all. She said she didn't know which one to pick, even after watching all her classmates receive affirmations that their answers were great. She said she didn't want to be wrong, even though there was absolutely no money at stake. I'd love to tell you that she was an exception, but I encounter many financial-coaching clients who won't even try to formulate their own answer before asking to be told what is the right one. I don't believe it's because they're not capable. I believe it's because their fear of failure outweighs their conviction to be financially free. These fears are likely created because of their upbringings. The good news is that this fear can be overcome, with awareness, safe spaces to practice, and repetition. I finally got her to pick one, and she let out a sigh of relief after I reassured her that her logic was sound. She knew the right answer for her, after all!

Fear of Success

If I'm being candid, I never really understood this fear until after I coached more and more first-generation women. Why would anyone be afraid of success? Isn't success awesome? But I learned that success has a high price for many people who are afraid to leave family and friends behind.

It's very hard to accept that even though you love someone, they may not want or be able to go on this journey of financial independence with you. I've heard from many students whose families shamed them for suddenly being "too good for them." In a podcast interview with one of my favorite Latina personal finance experts, Jannese Torres, she and I talked about the challenges of what we referred to as "wealth guilt." We were both among the first women in our families to achieve financial freedom, and we experienced the pitfalls of still belonging to a cultural narrative of scarcity. This situation can be extraordinarily complex, emotionally taxing, and sometimes even lonely.

But as mentioned in the Millionaire Moves in Chapter 1, those who are meant to be on this journey with you will rise to the occasion. What's been surprising and amazing is that many of the people who have continued to support me in my own quest for financial freedom are people I never expected to. My transparency in my own money struggles has actually brought me closer to certain people whom I wasn't close to before. I used to be self-conscious about the fact that I have a small social circle, but I've now realized that I'm incredibly lucky to have a handful of people in my corner who love me as I am.

Choose to Fight for Financial Independence

Which of these fears did you most relate to? The bad news is that it's unlikely you'll just "get over" these fears overnight. Fears are hard to erase—even as a millionaire, I sometimes find myself afraid of making financial mistakes. The good news is that even if they don't completely disappear, you can still become financially independent in spite of those fears. Recognizing and acknowledging your particular fear responses is the first step. It's totally normal to experience fears, but it's crucial not to let them paralyze you.

The one thing that I ask you to do is choose to fight these fears. Flight, freeze, fawn, and freak-outs won't make you rich. The habits we're going to start cultivating in Part 2 will help you find practical, hands-on ways to do that. If you think about all the freedoms that have been won over the course of history, all of them required someone to fight for them. And realistically, in a capitalistic and consumer-driven world, financial freedom won't come without you fighting for it either.

Now, fighting doesn't necessarily mean that you have to be aggressive or loud. You don't have to pick literal fights with people or work yourself to the point of burnout. It simply means acting intentionally and thoughtfully when your first instinct might instead be to flee, freeze, fawn, or freak out.

I asked my latest cohort of the CRUSH Bootcamp (which spans all ages and backgrounds) this question: How would you know you're fighting? What would the fighting spirit look like in you? These were some of the responses, which made me so proud of them:

- "I would not give a f*** what people think of me." —Sandra
- "I would push past procrastination and negative self-talk." —Beth
- "Writing down my wins and reflecting on them." —Victoria

- "When I'm able to articulate a response to any messaging not in line with my truth/goals." —Meghan
- "People are starting to notice what I am doing that is making me 'different' and managing money differently." —Brien
- "I'm uncomfortable. Which means I'm breaking bad habits." —Matthew

Reading this book can be your first declaration as a fighter for your financial freedom. Now that we've talked about the mistakes you're going to avoid in the future, let's get to the good stuff! In the next section, you'll learn how the power of habits can help you fight for financial independence.

Smart Habits Don't Require Thinking

A habit is a "settled tendency or an acquired mode of behavior that has become nearly or completely involuntary," according to the Merriam-Webster dictionary. Even more precisely, the *American Journal of Psychology* defines a habit as "a more or less fixed way of thinking, willing or feeling acquired through previous repetition of a mental experience." In other words, habits are mostly subconscious or even unconscious. A real habit often ends up being unintentional and requires little to no mental gymnastics. This is an important definition that most of us overlook when it comes to money. We're constantly being told that we need more knowledge, when what we really need is more practice: practice around building habits that last, not just habits that make us look good on social media or give us something to check off in our pretty planners.

And honestly, when it comes to money, we all have habits. Whether or not they are smart is another story. And I hope this book can help you start to shift away from the unconscious money habits that are no longer serving you toward more intentional behaviors. But as a money coach, I've learned that poor habits are hard to break, and even more importantly, good habits won't last if they are just stacked on top of bad ones.

One of the key things that I want you to understand right now is that my smart money habits are not complicated. They are designed to be simple so that you can eventually do them without thinking too much, or even at all. That's how you know you've successfully created a habit—when you've done the thing and don't even think twice about it! Here are the two other most important mental shifts you need to make to set yourself up for success with the habits in Part 2.

Mental Shift #1:
Swap Instead of Sacrifice

Repeat after me: *I do not need to sacrifice to be good with money.*

Do you believe me when I tell you that? Chances are, probably not, because of what you've heard before about personal finance. You know, the traditional budgeting mindset that says, "Cut back, deny yourself, and tighten those purse strings as much as humanly possible." Sound familiar? Sacrificing has been the go-to method for ages, but here's the kicker: That method often makes you feel like you're dragging a financial anchor.

You're saying no to those brunch dates, cutting out your daily latte, and living on the bare minimum. It's a disciplined approach, sure—but it sucks the joy out of your financial journey. Ever notice that feeling of resentment and frustration creeping in? Yeah, that's the sacrifice trap. Get out of that and try swapping instead.

Let's discuss the magic of swapping versus sacrificing when it comes to sculpting those money habits. As your millionaire money mentor on this journey to financial independence, I'm about to help you flip the script on how you view money management, forever.

I've been on more than thirty podcasts, radio programs, and television shows, and whenever they've heard about my payoff of $300,000, the question always comes up: What did you have to sacrifice to get there? In my earlier interviews, when I was still fresh off the debt payoff, I would respond with the usual, "We went down to one car instead of two. We sacrificed going out with our friends. We gave up alcohol. We didn't go on vacation for a while." Wow—look at me; I'm so virtuous and disciplined!

But now that I'm seven years into my debt-free journey, I realized that I actually swapped more than sacrificed. Now, that doesn't mean that I didn't give some things up, nor does it discount the work that I had to put in to make my goals a reality. More often, I was able to make a different decision that still aligned with my values but better prioritized my future freedom. Swapping is all about making choices that align with your goals without feeling like you're missing out on life. It's not about denying yourself or sacrificing everything; it's about consciously choosing joy in your budget now, and also for your future self. Take dining out, for example. Instead of "sacrificing" your favorite restaurant experience, call it a swap and have a fun-filled night of cooking at home. Or get takeout, which is less expensive than eating at a restaurant. Either way, you still get to savor delicious meals and stash away some savings. Frame the things you'll let go as a win-win!

As I was writing this book, I decided to make some swaps that would free up my time and energy to give this my best shot. Instead of planning our next international trip, AJ and I decided to replace it with road trips this year. It's saving us the cost of plane tickets and more expensive hotels. I've also stumbled across so many cute cafés from which I wrote these chapters! Sometimes, the swaps not only save you money but also create new adventures and memories that will surprise you!

The Positive Reinforcement Loop

What sets the swapping mindset apart? The positive reinforcement loop, my friends! When you swap out high expenses for lower-cost things that still light up your life, you create a cycle of positivity and reward. You'll have less financial guilt—and a sense of accomplishment and progress toward your goals.

When you use the swapping technique, you're building a relationship with money that's based on fulfillment and joy, not just pure discipline. The more you see those savings grow or inch closer to your financial dreams, the more motivated and excited you become. It's a beautiful cycle that keeps you on track without the emotional toll of cutthroat sacrifice.

Swapping Is Flexible and Customizable

Life's unpredictable, right? That's where swapping shines. The mindset of swapping also allows you to adapt gracefully to changes in goals or circumstances. For example, when I decided to finally quit my day job to take the risk of being my own boss, AJ and I swapped from two cars to one.

But the change felt well worthwhile, even if it meant being inconvenienced from time to time. Swapping lets you roll with the punches, adjusting your money moves as life throws curveballs your way. It's a flexible, personalized approach to budgeting that sets the stage for long-term success.

Swapping also encourages you to think about what's important to you. You're constantly asking yourself, "Does this spending align with my goals? Does it bring me joy?" This heightened awareness transforms your relationship with money, empowering you to make choices that resonate with your values and long-term vision. One of the most beautiful side effects of pursuing smart money habits is that you'll start to learn what actually matters to you—many of us just go through the motions and never think much about it. Even if it's difficult to swap certain things at first, you'll quickly realize the process is in service of a much happier, much healthier, and much wealthier you!

Mental Shift #2:
Get Bad Before You Get Good

Accept that you might not be great at managing finances at first, and that's okay. This topic is where I spend the most time coaching women on building smart money: just getting started. Many women assume that because I'm a money coach, I must have been good with money all along. But I got good with money because I started out being pretty terrible with money.

Why is this mental shift important? Because I realized that being bad at my financial plan meant that I actually had a plan. And starting the process meant that I was going through the part where I made mistakes and learned quickly from them.

I hate to break it to you, but there is no way you will make it through this financial independence journey without ever making a mistake or a move you'll regret. I often coach women who are totally stuck in their finances because they think that if they just build up enough confidence, they'll be motivated to do the hard things. But the only way I know to build confidence that will sustain you through your hardest time is to get used to being the worst in the room. If you only show up to rooms where you are the best, then you're not growing!

You might be giving up on building new habits because:

- They're hard.
- You feel like everyone else is better.
- You might look dumb.
- You might even be the worst in the room.

But if you don't push yourself, then how will you grow, sis?! Believe me, I know this feeling. I love to dance even though I will never be one of the best. I love hip-hop and I'm intimidated every damn time I show up for dance class. In one class I went to, I was objectively the worst dancer in the room. The others I was grouped with included one of the dance teachers, the owner of the studio, and another seasoned dancer. There I was, the girl who could barely remember an eight count even after trying it a dozen times. Am I a fool for continuing to show up?!

No! Because every time I do, I have fun, burn calories, and get slightly better than the try before. That day I was grouped with the pros, I took a deep breath and danced with them anyway. And it turns out I didn't die! The only person preventing your progress is you. Get (or dance) out of your own way! Stop letting your ego keep you from leveling up.

As you dive into the habits in Part 2, you'll probably be tempted to put off trying a new money habit until you find just the perfect time, or you're feeling super motivated to get going. Instead, remember that movement beats motivation every time. The more moves you make, the faster your progress will be, so commit to at least trying the habit instead of giving up before you even get started. You are ready for this!

RICH REFLECTIONS

When have you tried to avoid pain instead of choosing a potential gain? How did that affect your money habits?

Have you ever felt "wealth guilt" or fear of success? How did it manifest, and how did you cope with it?

Reflect on a time when you felt resentment or frustration from having to sacrifice something for your financial goals. How did it affect your willingness to keep practicing money habits?

Have you ever experienced a positive reinforcement loop in any area of your life? How can you apply this concept to your financial habits?

Think about a moment when you fought for your financial independence. What motivated you, and how did you feel afterward?

PART 2

THE POWER
OF SMART
MONEY HABITS

Now it's time to learn and attempt the twenty-five practical habits that you can use to create and maintain a budget, make smart spending decisions, and invest wisely. Financial freedom is not achieved by knowing what to do. It happens by doing what you need to do!

You don't have to commit to practicing all twenty-five habits right off the bat, but I encourage you to try at least one from each letter. Persevere through your mistakes and obstacles and remind yourself that they're proof you're moving forward! The CRUSH plan is built around simplifying your finances and focusing on what's most important to you. Each letter stands for a distinct step in building your financial-freedom plan:

C
is for CURATE Your Accounts:

This step involves organizing and streamlining all your financial accounts. Once you review every account you have, you'll gain an organized and uncluttered overview of your financial landscape. This awareness and simplification helps in tracking progress, optimizing savings, and building a solid foundation for financial growth without tedious spreadsheets.

R
is for REVERSE Into Independence:

Reverse engineering your path to financial independence means having a unique and compelling vision for your future life and setting clear, measurable milestones. Then you can work backward to identify the steps needed to achieve them. By understanding where you're heading and breaking down the journey, you will be able to create actionable plans, making the path to independence more manageable and even more fun.

U
is for UNDERSTAND Your (Net) Worth:

Understanding your net worth is crucial for financial freedom, yet most people don't even know their net worth. This step involves assessing everything you own and everything you owe, providing a comprehensive picture of your financial standing. Building monthly evaluation habits will empower you to make confident, informed decisions; avoid costly mistakes; and adjust strategies as you head into challenging times in your life.

> " *The intention to keep throughout your trials and errors is that you are* **learning to let your habits control your money** *instead of letting your money control your life.* "

is for SPEND Intentionally:

is for HEAL Your Money Wounds:

Spending intentionally sounds simple, but it's the step that gets most people tripped up. You'll focus on aligning your expenses with your financial-freedom goals, as well as with your dreams, values, and deeply rooted beliefs. This step encourages mindful spending by prioritizing physical and emotional needs over material wants and reprioritizing funds toward loving yourself not only now but in the future.

We all have money wounds. Some go back to our early childhoods, and we've been carrying them and leaving them wide open for decades. Healing your money wounds involves addressing and overcoming any negative beliefs or habits surrounding money. By fostering a healthy mindset, you create a positive foundation for making sound financial decisions and achieving lasting independence.

The steps appear in this order for a very intentional reason. I learned that many people's money plans go awry because they do the steps out of order, or skip steps altogether. To achieve sustainable financial independence, don't skip any steps, and recognize that all the steps are deserving of time and energy, even if your money narrative has told you otherwise up until now.

In the chapters ahead, I'll introduce you to each of the steps in CRUSH in greater depth, highlighting five tried-and-tested habits per step that will help you solidify smarter money behavior and work toward financial freedom. Don't forget that money notebook while you read so you can respond to the Rich Reflections prompts and journal your progress along the way. Then, share it with our online community at CRUSHYour MoneyGoals.com! Let's dive in!

3 Curate Your Accounts

The first step of the CRUSH plan is to curate your accounts—in other words, take inventory of the various bank accounts, credit cards, loans, and properties that you have in your name and simplify and streamline them to only the most necessary. Remember the key to CRUSHing your money goals is not multitasking and juggling a gaggle of accounts where you lose track of them easily. When it comes to achieving financial independence, the fewer accounts you have, the fewer opportunities for mistakes or precious money to fall through the cracks.

Think of each of your financial accounts as a separate handbag. Having multiple checking, savings, and investment accounts and credit cards is like carrying around an armful of handbags with just a little bit of money in each. It's not efficient and it feels a little silly (though it would be nice if they were all luxury!). Just as carrying all those bags would be a pain in the butt, having more accounts to manage than you really need can weigh you down financially and emotionally. Kicking a multitasking habit will take practice (I'm still working on it myself!), and the five habits in this chapter will help you focus your attention. You'll learn to slow down and reduce the number of financial accounts you're managing on a daily basis so you can significantly boost your financial progress without overcommitment and multitasking stress.

THE CURATED TWENTY:
Get Down to Twenty Accounts

The first and most important money habit to learn is to reduce the number of financial accounts you have down to twenty or fewer. Why twenty? I have seen so many people get overwhelmed with money management—and a big part of the problem is that they simply have too many accounts. When you try to overlay multiple goals over a disorganized list of dozens of accounts, it can get messy and confusing quickly. The four-step process to this habit will help you get ahold of what you have.

1. Gather Your Total Net Worth in One Secure System

Before tackling any financial goal—whether it's paying down debt, saving, or investing—it's important to understand how each account you own fits into your overall financial well-being. One way to measure your financial well-being is by determining your net worth. As a reminder, your net worth is calculated by taking the monetary value of everything that you own and subtracting out the monetary value of everything that you owe, including credit card debt, car loans, mortgages, student loans, and other forms of debt. The easiest way to get this data is to store all your accounts in one online system. In most systems, you will upload all your financial accounts securely so that everything is in one view. You can then link all your independent credit cards, loans, investments and cash accounts there too.

NET WORTH TRACKERS

Here are examples of online net worth trackers to gather all your financial accounts into a single tool.

- Monarch Money (what I use personally for a nominal monthly fee)
- Empower (free tool in the US, but be prepared for a sales pitch every now and then for your investments)
- PocketSmith (tool if you're based in Europe)

There are several online net worth trackers available that are easy to use, but you can sometimes also find a net worth tracker included in the dashboard of one of the banks you do business with already. I have not yet met a CRUSH Bootcamp member who has shown me a spreadsheet that works better than these systems. These tools reduce the busywork of updating manual spreadsheets (and are a lot less soul sucking and boring). For now, don't worry about how many accounts you have—simply get them all in one location.

It may be a pain to find all your usernames and passwords, but curating your accounts will help you see each account's relative impact to your finances. For example, $5,000 worth of credit card debt is more impactful to someone whose net worth is $50,000 versus $500,000.

2. Organize Your Accounts Into the "Financial Five"

As you bring your accounts into one platform, organize them into these five financial categories (these systems will often already do this for you):

1. **Cash and cash equivalents**, including checking, savings, certificate of deposit, money market, and similar accounts.
2. **Investments**, including retirement accounts, employer-sponsored accounts, brokerage accounts, and money in smaller investor apps such as Robinhood.
3. **Property**, including any property that could be liquidated for cash, such as your vehicles, real estate, art, or other items of value that you consider to be part of your wealth.
4. **Credit cards**, including ones that you may not actively use but are still open.
5. **Loans**, including student loans, personal loans, car loans, mortgages, medical debt, and tax debt. This category includes any debts you owe other than credit cards.

The first three categories are assets that will help you build your wealth and add to your overall net worth. The last two categories are liabilities and will detract from your overall net worth. By organizing all of your accounts in this way, you see the holistic picture of where all your money is. As you build better money habits, you can shift your attention and focus to the first three rather than the last two.

ACCOUNTING FOR YOUR MORTGAGE AND YOUR HOME EQUITY

Your mortgage is a loan that you owe to the bank, so it should be accounted for as a part of your net worth, since it's also likely to be your largest liability. Similarly, the market value of your home should be added to the calculation as it represents the amount of money you own for that piece of property. The equity in your home is another way of saying the net worth of your home. You can use real estate websites such as *Redfin* or obtain a comparative market analysis from a licensed real estate agent to help determine an estimate of your home value. As you organize your accounts, your mortgage will fall under your loans while your property value will fall under your property. Though these two line items are related to the same entity (your home), the home value is an asset and the mortgage is a debt.

3. Give Every Account a Meaningful Name and Distinct Purpose

As you review all of your accounts, really think about what it means to curate. Someone who curates is different from someone who collects, and most people collect money accounts rather than curate. Curation means you:

- Take special care and consideration of each account.
- Have a level of discernment beyond surface level.
- Have an intellectual curiosity about how to find the best accounts.
- Enjoy the process of accumulating them.
- Know which ones to let go of and when.

To that end, now go and edit the name of each account to reflect its purpose and how you feel about it. Names of your accounts should reflect your attitude and whether you want them to stay and grow (e.g., your retirement funds) or eventually go away (e.g., your loans). Be creative, clever, or just plain honest about what the accounts do for your wealth-building journey. Have fun with the names so that looking at your finances is more joy and less drudgery!

For example, here are some names members of my CRUSH Bootcamp and I have used for various accounts:

- "Bills, Bills, Bills" for your everyday checking account (this one is popular among my fellow millennials thanks to the Destiny's Child song)
- "My Dream Home" for money you're saving up to buy your next home
- "Sippin' Piña Coladas" for retirement savings
- "Let's Fly Away" for your favorite travel credit card

Get sassy! If you have accounts that don't elicit a smile, it's okay to acknowledge that. Name them in a way that reminds you of your intention to get rid of them! I named each individual loan some form of "Get out of here!" or "You'll be gone soon!" to keep me motivated even when I was hitting a payment plateau.

4. Close and Consolidate Until You Have Fewer Than Twenty Accounts

Naming each account uniquely helps you figure out if you have multiple accounts performing the same purpose and identify any that don't have a concrete purpose. Question why you have more than four accounts in any particular category.

For example, having more than one checking account is, more often than not, highly unnecessary and a missed opportunity to earn more interest. I also often encounter CRUSH Bootcamp members who have multiple savings accounts without saving for anything in particular, or just a blanket "just in case" account but not any real intention behind stashing that cash. Start with curating down to:

○ One checking account for daily expenses
○ One savings account for emergency funds (which we'll call a Keep Calm Fund; more on that later)
○ One savings account for a long-term savings goal
○ A business checking account (if you own a business)

Matthew Is Flying High with Less Baggage

Matthew is one of my most dedicated and committed students of all time. As a commercial pilot with a wife and young child, he came into my bootcamp and absolutely blew me away with his ability to reflect deeply and make changes quickly (though he will think they weren't fast enough).

"I am so glad I pulled the trigger and made the investment in myself and my family by purchasing and completing this bootcamp. Bernadette has given me the tools to lead my family to financial independence. My mindset about money has changed for the better.

"One of the things I took away is to give yourself time. It's going to take time to change your habits and thoughts around money; it won't happen overnight. I learned that I was holding on to too many financial bags, and once I started dropping some and carrying the ones that meant the most to me, things became easier.

"Another thing I took away is how to budget! I never learned an effective and easy way to budget, and Bernadette broke things way down for me and made budgeting really feasible. I'm excited to set monthly budget meetings with myself. This was a worthwhile experience. I love Bernadette's honesty and realism. She tells you how it is in a loving manner because she wants you to be successful! I'm grateful to be a part of this community of money CRUSHers! We have all our credit cards paid off. Next we're working on paying off our car loans, then my wife's student loans. My goal is to get our two car loans and her student loans paid off in the next two years! Let's go!"

Advanced investors may have more than four investment accounts, but if you're just beginning, you can start organizing them like this:

○ Consolidating taxable investment accounts, such as moving your Robinhood and Acorns accounts into one brokerage account, like Fidelity
○ Rolling over old 401(k)s into your current 401(k) for simplicity
○ Closing taxable brokerage accounts if you are not maximizing your retirement accounts
○ Recovering forgotten investment accounts

As you do this, it's a good idea to also review the expense ratios and fees of your investment accounts so you are aware of those amounts. I also commonly see students using taxed brokerage accounts to invest in the same things they could invest in with an account like a Roth IRA, which offers tax advantages.

RICH REFLECTIONS

On a scale from 1 to 10, how curated are your accounts right now? Why do you think you managed it that way up until now?

If you became a 10 in curation, what would that do for your confidence in managing your finances?

Are there any accounts that hold sentimental value? How can you honor that sentiment even if you close the account?

Did you notice a theme when you named your accounts? What do those names say about what your values are?

If your best friend saw the names of all your accounts, how would you feel? Would they say it matches who you are?

THE POWER OF WORLD PEAS:
Use the 80/20 Rule to Improve Your Financial Outlook

One of my favorite money habits started out a century ago in a pea garden. In 1906 Italy, there was a good-looking guy named Vilfredo Pareto (in a 1900s kind of way—seriously, google him!). He noticed that most of his precious pea plants would perish, except for a small portion. When he started counting plants, he noted that 20% of his crop produced 80% of his harvest.

Pareto extended this principle to macroeconomics, estimating that 80% of the wealth in Italy was owned by 20% of the population. Though the rule doesn't have scientific roots in it, it's accepted to be intuitively true. You probably now know it as the Pareto Principle or the 80/20 rule. I like to refer to it as World Peas (I crack myself up every time I say this)!

What does all this have to do with your financial outlook? You can use the 80/20 rule to find the 20% of your time, resources, and efforts that can yield 80% of the results or rewards in your money goals. This one principle completely transformed my ability to build and stick to good money habits and become a debt-free millionaire. It's particularly helpful if you're a perfectionist or an overthinker. Here's how you can apply the principle of World Peas to your money habits in three different ways.

Prioritize the 20% of Your Money Accounts That Will Produce the Most Return

The first way to apply the 80/20 rule is to look at your finances in the same way that Pareto looked at his peas. Instead of dedicating too much time to money accounts with minimal return, prioritize the 20% that have the most potential for gain.

How can you tell which are the 20% of your money accounts that can drive 80% of your success? Here are some ways to determine that:

- Identify one or two accounts out of the twenty you've curated that could materially change your financial situation.
- Identify the best 20% of your assets or investments, focusing on those that have the most potential for growth.
- Move those items you've been avoiding at the bottom of the list to the top. For example, if you've been avoiding paying off your credit card balances because it overwhelms you, dealing with it "later" usually means "never." Move it to the top of your list and tackle it before you attend to the other more comfortable items.
- Shift your focus to increasing your retirement accounts instead of just collecting credit card rewards.

You can also apply this idea to prioritizing what gets your attention in your budget each month. Ask yourself: *What are the two things this month that, if I really put my best effort in, would get me the biggest bang for my buck?* If you are like me and consistently overspend on food, set aside other priorities and focus your energy optimizing how you shop, plan, and prepare your meals. Set aside other priorities for this month (and potentially for the next few months) until you create a sustainable routine.

Ditch the 20% of Money Accounts Causing You the Most Drama

The second way to apply the 80/20 rule is to eliminate the 20% of your accounts that cause the most drama. It's time for some honest introspection—identify the 20% of your money accounts causing 80% of your money-related sleep loss. Eliminating these could reshape the trajectory of your financial future.

I refer to these stress-inducing accounts as the squeaky wheels in your financial plan. Rather than chipping away at them, little by little for years, focus on getting rid of them for good ASAP. Maybe it's the accounts with high interest rates or recurring bills you can't seem to ever fully pay off or that debt that you've avoided prioritizing. Perhaps it's the feeling you don't have enough savings. These squeaky wheels should be removed from your financial situation permanently.

Credit card debt is a squeaky wheel for many of my clients. They come to me because credit card debt has completely taken over their finances. In this example of using the 80/20 rule, consider your credit card debt as the squeaky wheel and state to yourself:

> *"If I pay down this credit card and keep my balance at zero permanently, I can improve the overall quality of my financial plan and my mental health."*

AJ Focused His Energy on Our Debt

When applying the 80/20 rule in the first year I pursued financial independence, my husband, AJ, and I focused our joint efforts on paying down debt. I'm super lucky to have a husband who believes in the CRUSH plan enough to go on the financial-freedom journey with me. Reducing my debt was the top priority of my overall financial plan—the 20% that I would focus on the most. It got the vast majority of my attention for a whole year, and AJ was supportive of me setting aside other financial priorities like saving for retirement and going on vacations. That may sound like a hard year, but in hindsight, using that intense focus to pay off $72,000 of student loans in one year instead of a decade meant that I never had to stress about student loan debt again. And AJ didn't have to stress about me being stressed!

I love applying the rule this way, because it can be challenging to focus on finding the things that will give you the best financial results, specifically if you're newly learning about finances or you're unsure or worried about investing. But it can be much easier to identify items in your financial plan that would relieve the most personal stress, even if tackling those first is not mathematically the most beneficial.

Remember That Perfectionists Never Experience Freedom

The last way to apply the 80/20 rule as a money habit is to repeat this: "Eighty percent is good enough."

Read that statement again, especially if you are a self-proclaimed perfectionist and are aiming for 100% every time. When you make a financial decision, you want it to be 100%, right? You're looking for 100% accurate, 100% safe. The truth is that financial freedom will be hindered by your need for perfection. Let's say you kept being a perfectionist and you actually reached the net worth that you calculated for financial independence. What do you think your anxiety level would be? How carefree would you really be? How bogged down by numbers and accuracy would you be versus savoring the relationships and the joy?

Oftentimes I see very smart, incredibly capable people stop budgeting, stop planning, stop moving forward with their financial-freedom plans because their mentality is all or nothing—they have to be perfect or they're a failure. This all-or-nothing mentality will likely lead you to nothing rather than all.

 Gina Focused on the Squeaky Wheel and Paid Off Her Wheels!

Gina paid off her Jeep in full after focusing for a year following the initial CRUSH Bootcamp. She focused on the squeaky wheel of her debt and became consumer-debt-free. She started the CRUSH journey in January, and by Christmastime she said, "My goal was to be under $10K owed by the end of the year, and between a three-paycheck month, a Christmas bonus, and insurance money from my motor scooter getting stolen, I was able to 10x my Jeep payment this month! I'll be in the millionaire bootcamp with you in no time! I am so ahead of schedule with my goals in working with you!"

By spring of the following year, her Jeep was paid off and she was able to resume her savings and investing at full speed. Best of all, she married her longtime boyfriend, and they were set up for a financial foundation that was debt-free!

Perfectionists never feel financially free. Humans do. As you go through the habits in this book and attempt to try some new things to move forward in your financial-freedom plan, remember the 80/20 rule. If you can only do 80%, consider that good enough—perhaps even great.

You will be amazed at how different your life can be if you let go of perfection in your money habits. Even doing a new money habit 20% more than you do now would still move you forward, right? Understand that achieving 100% perfection in personal finances is unrealistic. You will certainly fail at some things. I would even venture to say that with this book, you may only implement 20% of it. But it would be great if you gave 20% of this book your best effort!

RICH REFLECTIONS

Name three accounts that, if you focused on them, would create 80% of the best results in your financial plan.

Name three accounts that are causing you the most drama and draining your energy. What can you do to remove those accounts altogether, even temporarily?

What have you had an all-or-nothing mentality about? Has that served you well? Why or why not?

Is 80% good enough? What's the benefit of aiming for 80% instead of perfect?

How can letting go of perfectionism help you reach financial freedom and emotional peace?

THE KEEP CALM FUND:
Gift Yourself Thirty Days of Grace

I've always hated the term "emergency fund" and the traditional advice about it. When advising on how much to save for emergencies, financial experts often quote three to six months' worth of living expenses—or more, depending on your needs and goals. However, according to a 2024 Bankrate survey, 66% of US adults would be worried about having enough emergency savings to cover their immediate living expenses for the next month if they were to lose their job tomorrow.

As a financial coach, suggesting a six-month emergency fund to my students increased their feelings of hopelessness when they were already strapped for cash. Reaching six months of living expenses in your savings is even more difficult when inflation is high and interest rates on debt are rising. But on the other side of the spectrum, I found a surprising number of CRUSH Bootcamp members who saved up more than six months' living expenses—but they were afraid to use the excess money to increase their wealth. Whether you've already saved up for emergencies or plan to, consider the following money tips first.

Your Keep Calm Fund Buys You a Thirty-Day Grace Period

Before you worry about amassing six months' worth of savings, I strongly recommend you first focus on saving for one month (or thirty days) of expenses. I advocate for thirty days first because I've been on the other side of job layoffs. My first jobs were in human resources for several *Fortune* 100 companies during the 2008 financial crisis, and I was responsible for laying off hundreds of people. During those really tough conversations, many employees were offered severance payment to help bridge the gap to their next role, but that's not always the case.

I'll never forget the fear I saw in people's faces when they were told their jobs were going away. Expecting that one day I might be on the other side of the table, I always keep at least thirty days' worth of pay in savings. It's what I like to think of as paying myself severance, should I ever need it. Having that severance plan for myself helped me stay calm even as I watched my income go to zero during the COVID-19 pandemic. Much like severance pay offered by an employer, your personal severance plan is a goodwill gesture to ease the transition. That's why I call it my Keep Calm Fund instead of an emergency fund.

Store Your Keep Calm Fund in a High-Yield Savings Account

If you have a checking account, you might also have a savings account that came with it. The bank is probably paying you less than 1% in interest, so don't use that for your Keep Calm savings. Instead, put them in a high-yield savings account. It's easy to open, and it pays at least ten times more than a regular savings account, with all the same benefits. High-yield savings accounts keep your funds within easy reach, so it isn't too difficult to access them when you need to. Keeping your money here will let it earn some interest while shielding it from the ups and downs of things like the stock market. If you do need to pull physical cash from this account, many banks partner with local ATMs for little to no fees.

FIND ONLINE BANKS FOR HIGH-YIELD SAVINGS ACCOUNTS

A high-yield savings account is especially helpful if you're paying down debt or are a beginner investor. Most high-yield savings accounts have daily compounding, earning you interest on your money every day. Over the long run, this leads to more cash than you'd get in regular savings accounts that compound monthly. Knowing that you're earning interest each day can motivate you to put money into the account regularly.

High-yield savings accounts are almost exclusively available through online banks. Banks without physical branches have overhead costs that are much lower than those of traditional retail banks with brick-and-mortar locations. This allows online banks to offer better interest rates to customers and charge fewer fees or no fees at all. Many are names you might not have heard of. But online banking has also become more popular with established financial institutions that are looking to bring in more tech-savvy customers.

What to Consider When Saving in a High-Yield Account

First, check the banks that you already bank with and see if they have high-yield options. It will simplify your life if you can avoid having too many accounts in too many places. I also highly recommend checking customer service ratings online for the bank before opening an account. Since many online banks are newer institutions, they may not have comprehensive customer-service infrastructure should you run into any technical issues.

And as with all bank accounts, confirm the bank is insured by the Federal Deposit Insurance Corporation (FDIC), and don't keep more than the $250,000 that is the insurance limit per person, per FDIC-insured bank, per bank account type. For example, if you have two savings accounts at the same bank and the total between the two is higher than $250,000, you won't be insured for the amount above $250,000 in total. Replacing your traditional accounts with a high-yield option offers a no-stress way to start growing your thirty days of savings—and your passive income—with very little risk.

Then, Build Toward Three Months of Keep Calm Savings

The US Bureau of Labor Statistics reported the average American household spent about $72,967 a year, or $6,081 per month, in 2022. If you follow the rule of thumb of three to six months' worth of living expenses, based on that average, you'd want anywhere from $16,732 to $33,464 in your Keep Calm Fund—which is a very wide range. It's impossible to predict all the possible scenarios that would require you using your Keep Calm Fund. And it would certainly be helpful to have more cash on hand should something catastrophic like a major home repair or a medical emergency occur.

As you decide how much to save, it's important to ask yourself: *What else could I do to create more financial stability with the thousands of dollars sitting idly?* It's also important to consider if having too much cash saved creates complacency in your current financial or career position, versus taking a more proactive approach to grow your income.

INVEST IN A TOP-NOTCH RÉSUMÉ AND COMPETITIVE INTERVIEW SKILLS

One of the main reasons to have a Keep Calm Fund is security if you lose your income. As a former human resources professional, I witnessed laid-off employees who didn't even have a basic résumé to start their job search. And many others had résumés that were outdated and overcomplicated. People struggle to document their relevant experience and transferable skills, even at executive levels. And as a recruiter, I met many applicants who were not well prepared for competitive interviews—often rambling or unclear in their responses. Plus, there is a *lot* of competition for jobs nowadays. According to career services company Zippia, the typical corporate job opening receives 250 résumés, with four to six candidates called for an interview.

Even if you think your job is stable, one of the best tactics you can employ against an unexpected loss of income is to hire a professional résumé writer and potentially a career coach. These experts, when properly trained and vetted, can objectively improve your résumé and strengthen your interviewing skills before you absolutely need to look for a new job. While hundreds of dollars may feel like a lot to invest in a résumé, losing your income without a competitive résumé could cost you thousands.

Pay Off High-Interest Debt Instead of Hoarding Cash

Based on Federal Reserve data from 2022, 48% of all credit card users have carried a balance at least once. With the average credit card interest rate around 27% in July 2024, keeping a high balance of cash is losing you money if you are also holding on to credit card debt. You may hold on to cash savings because you're following advice you received from parents and traditional financial advisors to save money. But realistically those funds are deteriorating at a fast rate if you face credit card interest payments over time. If you are hoarding cash while maintaining credit card debt, it is smarter to pay down the high-interest debt as quickly as you possibly can.

TOOLS FOR BETTER MONEY HABITS

To help shift your habits, track your total net worth with online tools such as Monarch Money or Empower, as mentioned earlier. These tools holistically show you how high-interest debt is eroding your overall wealth. You can also use a credit card interest calculator to see exactly how much of your hard-earned money is being allocated toward interest versus principal payments. Integrating these two money habits will encourage you to hoard less cash and pay down your debt.

It Doesn't Need to Be an Emergency to Use Your Savings

I stopped referring to these savings as an "emergency fund" and instead refer to it as your "Keep Calm Fund" because I coached many students who were hesitant to use their savings even when there *were* emergencies. Remember Angela, the client who had her whole basement flood, and even though she had built her thirty-day savings, she still put the repair on a credit card? She was in the habit of not having cash on hand, but also she was so proud of building it up that she didn't want to use the money, even though the situation was exactly what the Keep Calm Fund is for!

It doesn't have to be a life-or-death situation to dip into this account. The habit I encourage you to form is to be okay with using your Keep Calm Fund when you need it—money is only useful when you spend it. The point of the Keep Calm Fund, aside from getting through times like losing your job, is to deal with unexpected occurrences even if they're not health or disaster related. It can be as simple as having an unexpected guest come from out of town, or making a mistake in your budget that you didn't account for.

The power is not in the amount of money, but in the amount of runway and freedom it gives you when you get confronted with an anxiety-inducing situation. Even if you don't have a plan right away, with your Keep Calm Fund, you have at least the next thirty days to figure one out. None of us can predict the future, but you can put yourself in a position to be more ready and able to stay calm as you decide your next steps.

RICH REFLECTIONS

Instead of an "emergency fund," what can you call your savings to help you calm down?

Are you maximizing your interest-earning opportunities with your savings accounts? How does the idea of making interest daily motivate you to save more?

If your primary source of income were gone tomorrow, what is your game plan? Write it down and keep it saved in your email in case you need to refer back to it.

Are you keeping money in cash even though you have debt to pay off? Why?

What challenges would you have in keeping at least thirty days' savings in your Keep Calm Fund as a habit? What can you do proactively to make this habit stick?

THE CREDIT CARD CRACKDOWN:
Pay Off Your Balance Weekly

Boy, oh boy, people love their credit cards. It's a point of constant debate between me and other financial experts who tout the glories of credit cards. When I first became a money coach, I falsely assumed that every person who had credit card debt was a frivolous spender. It turned out that many CRUSH Bootcamp members had accumulated credit card debt after years of being responsible credit card holders. All it took was a one-time emergency— one job loss, one huge medical expense, or one major car repair—to create a growing mound of debt that they could not get out from under.

Between 2022 and 2023, average credit card balances grew by 10% to $6,501, according to Experian data. When interest rates rise, even if you're not spending any more on a credit card, not being able to pay off your full balance on time may mean that the balance will grow faster than you can keep up with. A 2023 consumer research study revealed that 45% of consumers with credit cards carry balances month over month. So, no—I don't think credit cards and their point systems are the ticket to wealth.

Don't worry, I'm not going to suggest you quit credit cards completely. Dubbed the Credit Card Crackdown, this habit encourages you to be honest and critical about your credit card use—and how reducing your dependence on them can lead you to financial independence faster. As we work through this habit, you'll gain a better understanding of the mindset credit cards instill in you—and how pausing them for a while can stabilize your finances. When you begin using them again, make it a goal to pay off the balance every week, not just when they are due. It is important to start each new calendar month with a clear slate if you want to accumulate wealth in dollars, not just points.

The Truth about Credit Cards

While we know that high interest rates can negatively impact wealth, the costs of credit card spending are not as obvious for those who pay their balances in full every month. When I stopped using credit cards altogether for nearly five years, there was a clear difference in how much I spent, how often I shopped, and how expensive the items were that I chose to buy. Before you can build a healthy credit card habit, here are key pieces of knowledge to consider.

Credit Cards Make You Spend More on Higher-Priced Items and Impulses

According to MIT psychology researcher Drazen Prelec, "People tend to spend more when using credit cards than cash. Not only are they more likely to buy something at a higher price, they also are likely to give larger tips and make more impulse buys."

A study by the *Journal of Consumer Research* also showed that people who pay using a more tangible form of payment, such as cash, increase their connection to the product after the purchase in comparison to those who pay with less painful forms of payment, like credit cards. If you are someone who is prone to impulse purchasing, removing the availability of a credit card can create a mindset of spending only when you've carefully considered why.

Credit Scores Tell If You Love Borrowing Money, Not Managing It

We are misled to believe that having a decent credit score is critical to building wealth. I won't deny that there are certainly benefits to having a high credit score: lower interest rates on large purchases, easier approval for buying or renting a home, and higher limits on credit cards. But most people don't keep track of their credit score until they want to make a major purchase, and even fewer know how credit scores are calculated. Before you stress about boosting your credit score, learn what this number truly measures about you and your money.

In 1989, the Fair Isaac Corporation debuted FICO scores to provide an industry standard for assessing whether or not a consumer would be a good candidate for a loan. A FICO score is the three-digit number, based on the information in your credit reports, that helps creditors determine how likely you are to pay back their money. This, in turn, determines how much you can borrow, how many months you have to repay, and how much they will charge you in the form of an interest rate.

A lot of financial education rhetoric says credit scores are an indicator of financial health. However, that isn't always the case, because this number does not take into account other important factors. Creditors just want a fast, brainless way to decide whether or not to loan you money, and the FICO score provides that. In most cases, they'll only look at your FICO score and won't pay as much attention to the report details. By having a quick, easy way to determine loans, banks save a ton of money in salaries. They can hire less-skilled workers who simply input the data and have the system spit out a score, instead of qualified underwriters who actually analyze the data. A common myth is that your income is a consideration in determining your credit score—it's not. Other items *not* included in your credit score are:

- Job history
- Cash savings
- Property that you own
- Investments

As a financial educator, I've met a lot of new CRUSH Bootcamp members whose goal is to have an 800 credit score. And if they have a low credit score, it makes them feel like they've failed. Not only is it possible to be financially stable without a sky-high credit score; it's actually more likely for someone to have a top credit score if they have a stronger relationship with debt than with moderation. Your FICO score should not be your main measure of financial stability. It measures how good you are at borrowing money, not managing it.

Factors That Go Into Calculating Your Credit Score

Not all credit scores are FICO scores. Other kinds of credit scores can be very different from FICO scores—sometimes by as much as 100 points. Don't wait until you need your credit score to understand how it's calculated. You'll notice credit scores are entirely based on your relationship

with debt, not your finances as a whole. According to FICO, the five com-
ponents of a credit score are:

- **Payment history of your debts (35%):** Whether or not you get
  your payments in on time accounts for more than a third of your
  credit score. Making your payments on time, even if they're minimal, drastically improves credit scores.
- **Debt amounts owed (30%):** The total amount you owe across your
  accounts is next in importance to your score. Banks want to make
  sure you don't have so many other debts that you're at risk of coming up short on their loans.
- **Length of debt history (15%):** This refers to how long you've been
  making payments on your debt accounts. The longer you have a
  debt, the longer the history.
- **Mix of debts (10%):** How many different kinds of credit do you
  have? Banks like to see that the credit you have is coming from
  different places, like a mortgage and car payment, and not all on
  credit cards.
- **New requests for debt (10%):** How often are you asking to borrow
  money? Though many people think opening new accounts or getting credit checks is a big impact, it has much less influence than
  the other data points.

Shift Your Credit Card Focus from Accumulating Points to Accumulating Investments

Credit card companies have convinced us that they are helping us with
"points," when in actuality those points usually come at a significant cost:
your financial freedom. Points are designed to encourage you to spend
more money, not save or invest it. Focusing on spending money versus
investing money will naturally make financial freedom harder to achieve.

I will admit that I also used to be enamored with the idea of getting
points just for spending on my regular purchases. Credit card marketing
does a great job of making you feel like you are missing out if you're
not gaining all these seemingly free rewards in the form of flights, hotels,

and cash back. But once I stopped paying attention to my credit card points, I shifted to learning how to invest in real assets, such as dividend-producing exchange-traded funds, real estate investment trusts, and interest-bearing options like high-yield savings accounts and certificates of deposit.

COMPARING CREDIT CARD CASH BACK TO INVESTMENTS

You might be skeptical that managing credit card points isn't a great use of your time, as many people are. So, I showed my CRUSH Bootcamp some real-life numbers. In the first four months of 2023, I calculated how much I earned in credit card bonuses, and it amounted to $154.21. But the amount I accumulated in investing resulted in $10,005.27.

Are Credit Cards *Really* Helping You?

Many of my financial education students find it difficult to stay on a budget when actively using credit cards, and not only because they are spending more. Their expenses not only become more unpredictable, but depending on when their credit card bills are due, they find themselves short on cash for other items not charged on their cards.

You will find it significantly easier to fix your monthly budget and maintain it when you pause your credit card use—even temporarily—until you get into more sustainable money habits with savings and investments. Once you run out of cash allotted to various budget line items, you have no choice but to wait until the following month. You can also pay off your balance in full at the end of each week as opposed to paying it on the due date the credit card company assigned to you. That way, you can more easily see how much was spent from your current budget versus carryover from a previous month.

Even better, paying off your credit card balance every week will ensure you don't run low on cash balances by surprise. This forces you to still feel a little more of the true amount of spending versus letting a whole month go by between making the purchase and paying for it. You can also time your budget and payments by calling your credit card company and asking to change the due dates to align with your other expenses. There is no penalty for paying your credit card balances early.

While I don't expect you to quit credit cards altogether, I do challenge you to honestly assess if they are truly improving your ability to become financially independent in the long run. The bottom line is to have a habit of keeping two credit cards at most and getting to a zero balance at the end of every week, not just on the due date. I've met tons of people who have multiple credit cards—the most I've seen was twelve different cards, and their financial situation was not good.

I only have two credit cards in use, one for business and one for personal, and I've consistently had an 800 or higher credit score. You don't need lots of cards to build a good credit score, but you do need to control your credit card usage if you want to truly reach financial freedom.

RICH REFLECTIONS

Review your last credit card statement. Looking at each of those transactions, would you have spent more or less if you had to pay for them with paper dollar bills?

Do you use your credit card as an emergency fund? What could you do instead to reduce your risk?

If you were to keep one credit card, which would it be and why?

Try pausing your credit card use for one calendar month. Journal what changes you notice in your cash and in your spending.

Imagine if you were as excited about investing as you are about credit card points. How much more could you grow your wealth?

THE ANNUAL AUDIT:
Avoid the Insurance Racket

This last habit may not sound sexy, but it's absolutely worth the effort! And it's the part of a financial plan that many people avoid—insurance. The Annual Audit asks you to check in on what insurance you have and what you might need. Done once a year, this habit can save you tens, if not hundreds, of thousands of dollars over your lifetime. It's not the most exciting topic, and many of us don't fully understand how it even works. You've probably already purchased some sort of insurance in your lifetime, but what have you actually bought into? I used to not really know the answer to this question, even when I was working for one of the biggest insurance companies in the world!

Insurance is simply a formal way to manage your financial risks. When you purchase insurance, you are essentially purchasing protection against potential financial losses. The insurance company pays you (or someone you choose) if something bad happens. And if you have no insurance when an accident happens, you may be responsible for all related costs. Generally, we all know that insurance is an important part of our financial plans, but very few people pay particular attention to what they've actually purchased in their various insurance policies. That's why this is a really important habit for you to cultivate over the course of your lifetime.

As you may have noticed, I freaking love using acronyms. This annual-insurance-audit habit breaks down into five steps, spelling out "AUDIT."

A: Assemble Your Documentation

The first step is "A," assemble your policies and documents every year. You'll need to schedule around four hours to gather all your insurance policies, from the booklets to the receipts, in a safe spot and double-check them. Normally, I'm all about going digital, but keeping all my insurance policies in paper form makes it easier for me to read, highlight, and underline important parts. I keep them in my safe along with my other important documents, so when I have a stressful situation where I must file a claim, I don't have to rummage around or remember my username and password to find out what my insurance covers.

ASK ABOUT COVERAGE DURING JOB INTERVIEWS

I highly recommend that you do not wait until *after* you accept a job to learn what the health coverage is going to be. As you are going through an interview process, ask early on for the coverage information for health insurance and life insurance offered by the employer to determine if it is going to have a significant impact on your regular paycheck.

What about Life Insurance?

I want to address life insurance because it's one of the most common questions I get. First, life insurance can be important if you have dependents who are reliant on your income. However, I've coached clients who purchased a life insurance product with the intent of it being an investment vehicle—meaning, they were told by an insurance sales representative that it would help them grow their wealth. But they were often single women who had no dependents, and they could have taken the same money and put it into real investments, such as stocks, bonds, or real estate, that would have been more liquid in cases where they needed to pull out the money.

Many financial advisors sell life insurance products as investments, when in fact they are not. Even if they were, life insurance policies typically have lower returns than actual investments. Life insurance's primary purpose is to protect the people you love in the case of a financial loss. It does not protect you, nor is it an asset because it doesn't help you grow your wealth. There are two main types of life insurance—whole and term. Whole life insurance covers you for your entire life, with fixed premiums and a cash-value component that grows over time. It's more expensive because it provides lifelong protection and can be used for long-term financial planning. Term life insurance covers you for a specific period, with lower premiums and no cash value. It's more affordable and straightforward, often chosen for temporary needs like covering a mortgage or providing for dependents in case you pass away.

I personally do not recommend whole life insurance products. I think they are a total racket because they are usually highly complex and lack transparency, and the policies are very difficult to understand. I have also coached many clients who tried to cancel their whole life insurance policies and were not able to recoup any of the money they put into them. What's more, whole life insurance policies tend to have large commissions and fees that incentivize insurance agents to sell you higher-premium policies that you don't necessarily need. Now, I'm not saying that insurance agents are bad people! They are just doing their job. But it's your job—pursuing financial freedom—to make sure you ask the right questions and make a choice that's right for you.

I urge you, if you are someone who is currently carrying life insurance, consider term life insurance over whole life insurance. And more importantly, ask yourself the question: *Do I want to insure my death, or do I want to pursue financial freedom in the present while I'm still alive?* By asking yourself this question, you can decide if life insurance is even necessary or if you'd rather prioritize paying down debt, saving, or investing before purchasing life insurance.

U: Understand Your Coverage

The second step of your AUDIT, the "U," is to understand your coverage and your costs. You don't need to become an insurance expert; however, it's important to read the fine print and review all the coverage limits for your insurance plans, the actual costs, and the parameters by which you are paying. Specifically, assess the premiums, the deductibles, and the overall policy costs. One of the biggest pains that my clients experience is assuming that they have costs covered only to find out there is a high deductible. Or even worse, that their accident isn't covered at all.

The deductible is the amount that you will need to pay for covered services before your insurance plan will start to do its job. For example, if you have a $2,000 deductible, you must pay the first $2,000 of covered services yourself. Only after you pay that deductible in full do you start getting insurance money for the remaining expense.

PREMIUMS VERSUS DEDUCTIBLES

There is an inverse correlation between the amount of premium you pay and the deductible amount. In other words, a higher deductible usually means that you pay a lower premium. For example, the lower monthly or biweekly payments that you pay toward your premium, the higher the deductible amount is compared to other insurance plan options. The insurance company is going to get its money from you one way or another, whether it's collecting higher premiums from you up front or requiring you pay a higher deductible when a claim arises.

D: Determine Discounts

The "D" in AUDIT stands for discover discounts. This is where the Annual Audit is most valuable (and the most fun)! Once a year, call at least two other providers for each type of insurance you have and compare potential discounts and bundling opportunities. This step is where me being Filipino has really come in handy. Remember, few Filipinos are afraid to ask for discounts. It's our love language! Take this opportunity to share your current costs with other providers and simply ask if you can get a better rate for similar coverage. Also, check if any of the affiliations or organizations that you belong to—such as your employer, church, or societies—offer discounts as part of their member benefits. I once got a 25% discount on my home and auto insurance because I'd become a member of my college honor society years prior.

QUOTE OTHER PRICE LEVELS

During our Annual Audit, my husband requests quotes for the prices of the coverage levels directly below and above our desired level. For example, if we estimate we need loss coverage of $500,000, then we ask for quotes on the $300,000 and $750,000 coverage costs within the same provider. He once found going to the higher coverage was less than $10 more per six months, so it was worth the upgrade. Comparing the costs and benefits will help you make an informed decision.

I: Investigate Customer Service

The "I" in AUDIT stands for investigate customer service. Check your current providers on the Better Business Bureau or other similar customer-review sites and see how they have been rated in the past year. Evaluate how they respond to customer claims and the satisfaction ratings regarding claims processing and overall customer service.

Beyond that, actually test it out for yourself during your Annual Audit. I like to pretend I'm a secret shopper and call the customer-care numbers of each of my insurance providers and ask about my policy. See how you like their responses, treatment, and call wait times. The last thing that you want after you've been in a car accident or experienced a medical emergency is to be put on hold for hours. Take a few minutes to test if their customer-response times are acceptable. Speaking directly to your insurance agent can help you make an informed decision about their service levels.

Kevin Checked for Future Changes in Coverage

If you know there is a major change that's coming up that could impact your budget, plan ahead of time during your audit. For example, my CRUSH Bootcamp member Kevin was considering moving from North Carolina to California. He took the extra time to call insurance agents in California to determine what their rates would be for his renters insurance and auto insurance. It turned out his payments would be much higher in his new location, and this knowledge helped him plan how much money he needed to save in order to make the move, reducing a lot of the unexpected costs that could have surprised him and his partner when they arrived at their new home!

T: Tailor to Your Needs

Lastly, the "T" in AUDIT is all about tailoring your policies to your changing needs. Reassess your coverage needs based on life changes and major events you experienced in the past year. For example, if you had a child or are considering having a child, if you're getting married or divorced.

If you're adding new members to your household, or if the members of your household have turned a certain age, their coverage might be higher or lower. Consider if you've had any major repairs or damages or renovations to your home that might affect your insurance coverage.

As you find any of these changing needs on an annual basis, it is a perfect time to consult with your insurance agents. Discuss adjustments and make updates to find the appropriate amount of coverage for you and make sure you're benefiting the most from the premiums that you are paying.

RICH REFLECTIONS

Estimate how much you spent in total on all insurance premiums last year. Was it more or less than you thought? Do you feel it's "worth it"?

Pick three of your insurance plans to investigate for discounts. What questions do you have for your agents? Write them down.

Do you have any life events coming up that will change your insurance needs, such as moving to a new home, adding members to your family, or making upgrades to your property? What should you ask your insurance agents about these changes?

What organizations do you belong to that might offer insurance discounts? Are there other ways you can lower your premiums, such as doing a health exam or taking a defensive-driving course, and can you commit to doing so?

How can you reframe your insurance as an unsexy-but-necessary part of your journey to financial freedom with words of affirmation? For example, "This expense helps protect me and what I've built."

4 Reverse Into Independence

Remember, this book is not just about what you need to know. It's about what you need to *do* to reach financial independence and *win* the game of money. The second letter in CRUSH, "R," stands for reverse into independence—in other words, figure out your financial independence number, then determine the milestones you need to reach to make freedom a reality.

When I was starting out, financial independence and a comfortable retirement felt incredibly out of reach for me as a first-generation Filipino American. Perhaps, as used to be the case with me, you have never personally met someone who has successfully retired with enough money, let alone retired early. My own fears of retirement were hugely influenced by my immigrant father being forced into retirement by the advertising company he'd dedicated decades of long hours to. I personally witnessed my father's sense of identity slip away in retirement, as his job title was a big indicator that he had achieved success. Watching him feel lost woke me up to the realization that even if I loved my job, my sense of self-worth shouldn't be tied to something that could be taken away from me so easily.

Even if early retirement isn't a goal of yours, consider what the idea of financial independence means to you. Financial independence can mean having more agency over how you live your life—for example, whether you choose to continue working full-time or pivot and push rest and rejuvenation higher up on your priority list. It can mean not having to ask permission to go on vacation. It can mean spending more time with the people you miss most right now. What's been beautiful and inspiring about coaching the CRUSH Bootcamp is that no two members' definitions have been exactly the same!

These next five habits can help you reverse into a financial-freedom plan, using the same habits that helped me become debt-free (including paying off my home mortgage by age thirty-four). They can lead you toward becoming financially healthy and, more importantly, financially independent, however that feels most joyful to you.

I've intentionally shared these next five habits in the order that I find most optimal. Resist the urge to skip around and try implementing each habit before moving on to the next to increase your odds of success. You must also consciously balance and rebalance them to feel true freedom—not just financially, but mentally and emotionally too. Let's get to them!

THE CASH FLOW CUSHION:
Escape Paycheck-to-Paycheck Living

It's rough out there, my friends, and you are not alone! Approximately three in four Americans live paycheck to paycheck, per a 2023 Payroll.org survey. Studies like this one indicate that so many people find it challenging to save or invest money after paying their living expenses. If you are living paycheck to paycheck, it's nothing to be ashamed of.

People in these situations hear again and again that they need an emergency fund. It's long been hailed as a crucial safety net, providing peace of mind in the face of unexpected expenses or income disruptions. We talked in Chapter 3 about reframing your emergency fund as your Keep Calm Fund to give yourself thirty days of grace when unexpected situations arise.

But a different layer of financial security that's often overlooked helped me move on from the paycheck-to-paycheck cycle and become a debt-free millionaire: the Cash Flow Cushion. It's also a key component I teach as a financial coach to help my CRUSH Bootcamp save and invest more money toward financial independence. The Cash Flow Cushion is a lesser known but equally vital component of financial stability as the Keep Calm Fund. Here's what you need to do to make it a money habit for life!

How the Cash Flow Cushion Differs from Your Keep Calm Fund

"Living paycheck to paycheck" is a commonly used phrase, but it doesn't necessarily mean you lack income. In fact, I've coached many people who earn multi-six figures—at least $200,000 per year—and still live paycheck to paycheck! The expression more so represents a potential challenge: If you didn't receive your next paycheck for any reason, you would experience a significant amount of financial or emotional stress.

A Cash Flow Cushion is a buffer of funds that are readily accessible in your checking account and equal to one month's worth of expenses. Unlike a Keep Calm Fund, which is reserved for major unexpected expenses like medical bills or car repairs, the Cash Flow Cushion serves a different purpose. It's there to ensure you're not living paycheck to paycheck, providing financial and emotional stability and security in your day-to-day life. To start off, your Keep Calm Fund and your Cash Flow Cushion should each equal one month's worth of expenses. The Cash Flow Cushion will sit in your checking account as your buffer for everyday expenses and to move you out of the paycheck-to-paycheck cycle. The Keep Calm Fund is to be used for largely unexpected expenses outside of your normal expenses, while your Cash Flow Cushion is used every month to pay for expected expenses.

Determine How Much to Put in Your Cash Flow Cushion

To build a Cash Flow Cushion, start with a clear understanding of your monthly expenses. Calculate the total amount you typically spend in a month, including these five necessities:

- Rent or mortgage
- Utilities
- Food
- Transportation
- Essential health expenses like prescriptions or therapy sessions

Identifying these nonnegotiable expenses lays the foundation for determining the size of your cushion. Once you have a clear total of your typical monthly expenses, start setting aside funds to cover one month of them. This might involve reallocating some of your savings or adjusting your budget to prioritize building your Cash Flow Cushion.

Maintaining a Cash Flow Cushion requires intentionality and commitment—you must be dedicated to keeping the cushion at a level at which you can pay your bills each month without relying on your next paycheck.

Monitor your expenses at least quarterly to ensure your Cash Flow Cushion remains sufficient to cover your monthly expenses. If you encounter unexpected expenses or experience a temporary drop in income, be proactive about replenishing your cushion as soon as possible to maintain its effectiveness. Many checking accounts will allow you to set an alert when your balance reaches below a certain threshold. If one month's worth of expenses for you is $5,000, aim to always have at least $5,000 in your checking account and alert yourself if it goes below that. If it does drop below, it's an indication to you that you may need to temporarily scale back spending until it reaches over the threshold again.

BUT WHAT ABOUT INVESTING?

Despite its benefits, some people may be hesitant to prioritize a Cash Flow Cushion. Worrying about missed investment opportunities or low interest rates on checking accounts may deter you from allocating funds to your cushion. Usually, when people are hesitant about putting money in a Cash Flow Cushion, it's because they "heard" they could make more money by investing and/or they are listening to generic advice without thinking about the risk tolerance necessary to become a great investor. But hear me on this. To become a great investor, you must not be in the paycheck-to-paycheck cycle. Investing requires consistency, and the Cash Flow Cushion creates the consistency you need on a monthly basis for your everyday expenses.

I've personally witnessed dozens of people in my CRUSH Bootcamp who fell into the trap of investing before they actually had a secure Cash Flow Cushion and then found themselves running short on cash to pay their everyday expenses. Or even worse, they had money in investments while letting even more money leak in the form of high interest rates on their credit cards. Without a Cash Flow Cushion, you increase the risk of not having enough cash to pay your daily expenses, even if you have that amount of money sitting in investments.

Cash Flow Cushion Is the Bomb Dot Com

Yes, I know I aged myself with that phrase, but I'll never stop using it. The financial security your Cash Flow Cushion provides far outweighs any potential drawbacks. It breaks the mental cycle of waiting for your next paycheck to pay the bills you inevitably have due next month. It starts to put space between your survival instinct and your ability to think more strategically, so you can focus time and energy on more sophisticated financial goals like investing. Here are some other benefits of the Cash Flow Cushion:

It Lowers Your Stress Levels

One of the Cash Flow Cushion's most significant advantages is the reduction of financial stress. Knowing you already have next month's expenses covered provides peace and confidence to stop acting like you're broke. By prioritizing, creating, and maintaining a one-month cushion in your checking account, you can break free from the paycheck-to-paycheck mentality and enjoy greater flexibility, security, and the peace of mind of a future millionaire.

It Helps You Manage Smaller Financial Surprises

Additionally, a Cash Flow Cushion acts as a safeguard against expense fluctuations and income disruptions. Whether it's a larger utility bill or a temporary reduction in work hours, having that extra month of money readily available to pay your bills can help you bridge the gap without resorting to credit cards or loans.

It Smooths Out Irregular Income

A Cash Flow Cushion provides flexibility when you're managing irregular income and has helped me make my expenses so much easier to manage, especially as I grew my business from scratch. For freelancers, entrepreneurs, or anyone with fluctuating income streams, having this cushion in your checking account can help smooth out the highs and lows, ensuring you can cover your expenses during lean months without dipping into your Keep Calm Fund or accruing extra debt.

The CRUSH Bootcamp Invented the Cash Flow Cushion!

As a financial educator, I found my bootcamp clients facing a common challenge—the struggle to transition from living paycheck to paycheck to adopting a proactive budgeting approach. Repeatedly, I encountered inquiries from individuals grappling with the concept, unsure of how to break the cycle of financial instability. It was during these interactions that I realized the need for a practical solution to address their concerns and pave the way toward better budgeting habits.

Enter the CRUSH Bootcamp—the name affectionately bestowed upon my mentees who consistently attend a monthly meeting on navigating their finances. These awesome humans, united by their determination to conquer financial challenges, inadvertently became catalysts for innovation in my teaching approach. Their collective questions and shared experiences illuminated a crucial gap in financial literacy: the absence of a tangible strategy to bridge the gap between paycheck cycles and bills.

The concept of the Cash Flow Cushion was born—a simple yet powerful shift designed to provide them with a proactive remedy against unexpected expenses and income disruptions and, more importantly, to remove the paycheck-to-paycheck mentality. Its implementation offered newfound flexibility in managing irregular income streams, empowering them to navigate the peaks and valleys of their cash flow, and was particularly helpful in guiding the CRUSH Bootcamp through the uncertainty of the COVID-19 pandemic.

As you witness the transformative impact of the Cash Flow Cushion on your own financial-freedom journey, its significance will become undeniable. Once you introduce it into your monthly money routine, you may feel the light bulbs going off in your mind about why you haven't been able to budget effectively before. More importantly, this habit will help you kick off your financial independence plan with less confusion and more confidence than ever before.

RICH REFLECTIONS

Reflect on your current financial situation: Do you feel like you're living paycheck to paycheck, and if so, what steps have you taken to address this challenge?

Reflect on your attitudes toward financial security: How might having a consistent Cash Flow Cushion impact your overall financial well-being?

How much money do you need in your Cash Flow Cushion? Does that feel high or low?

What bills can you lower or get rid of so that your Cash Flow Cushion can be lower too?

Why do you deserve a Cash Flow Cushion? Remind yourself of how it aligns with your goals for financial independence and stability.

THE CHA-CHING CHECKLIST:
Five Questions to Stay Focused Every Month

You probably already know that keeping a budget can help you offset some of the squeeze you feel on your daily expenses. But have you tried to create a budget before and haven't been able to stick to it? According to a survey by Credit.com, 27% of Americans don't think they need a budget. And that's true. You don't need a budget...unless you want to be great with money, stop stressing about finances, and be able to claim financial freedom someday! Or you're a nepo baby who doesn't ever need to worry about money.

For the rest of us who are working hard to earn financial independence, here are five questions to habitually ask yourself every month. It's what I call the "Cha-Ching Checklist"! Use these as prompts at the start of every month to strengthen your wealth mindset and maintain a budgeting habit that can last you a lifetime. One of my most thoughtful CRUSH Bootcamp members, Meghan, shared, "I've come to really enjoy budgeting since following your methodologies, and I'm excited to incorporate this checklist to keep me more focused and efficient with my time (avoiding busywork)!"

1. Have I Scheduled Uninterrupted Time and Energy to Conquer My Budget?

The top reason CRUSH Bootcamp members tell me they can't budget is they are too busy. However, a solid budgeting routine, once implemented and practiced over a six-month period, will only take an hour or two a month. That's a small amount of time compared to the 3.1 hours per day the average American spends streaming video (guilty as charged, here!).

You can kick off your new budgeting routine with momentum by pulling out your calendar right now, whether it's on paper or online. Set up a recurring "meeting" with yourself and make it nonnegotiable, undisturbed time. Schedule the meeting for the same day and same time every month for one hour, maybe two as you're starting out. Put your friends and family on notice that you are booked and busy budgeting!

TAKE ONE STEP TOWARD KICKING OFF YOUR BUDGET

Having a hard time getting started during this allocated time? Try doing just *one* task to improve your finances for the month and see where it takes you! Here are some ideas:

- Call that dreaded customer-service line for the bill with a mistake that you've been meaning to get fixed.
- Pay off one credit card bill in full.
- Move some money from your checking account to your high-yield savings account to build your Keep Calm Fund.
- Close an account you no longer need.
- Journal on what caused you financial stress this month (using the Rich Reflections in this book!).
- Research that financial topic you've been meaning to finally understand.

Notice that this first of five questions asks if you scheduled time *and* energy to conquer your budget. I often find that people don't budget consistently because they're choosing a "meeting" time where they are at their lowest energy level. The worst time to plan this meeting is after a busy workday when you are stressed and tired. Instead, choose a consistent time and serene place where you can focus on your budget completely uninterrupted for up to two hours.

One of my successful CRUSH Bootcamp members, Jasmine, shared, "I love how energy is considered into this because it makes such a difference! As of now, my monthly time will be the last Thursday of the month for the next month (it's right before a paycheck and has the bonus of oncoming weekend vibes)! Already loving and enjoying this process!"

My husband, AJ, and I only take an hour to plan our monthly budget. We've kept that meeting at 5 p.m. on the first Sunday of every month since 2016. We tried during the week, but with both of us working full-time, we often carried our work stress into our meetings. That was definitely not going to help us keep levelheaded while making decisions together.

On Sundays, we typically spend the day reorganizing, relaxing, and getting ready for the coming week. I actually look forward to this time with my husband. It makes me feel in control of our lives. Keeping this uninterrupted budgeting time every month is the one habit I singularly credit for helping us pay off $300,000 of debt. If you want to stick to a budget every month, a regular schedule is key. Use this time to remove the clutter you've been meaning to clean up in your list of curated accounts.

2. Am I Focused on the Present? Or Am I Wasting Time Trying to Predict the Future?

Roughly three in four Americans reported feeling anxious about their financial situation in a 2020 Mind Over Money survey by The Decision Lab and Capital One. I learned from the CRUSH Bootcamp that we spend a lot of time trying to predict the future by reading countless articles, researching what might happen, and getting caught up in the financial news cycle.

The problem is that predicting the future is futile, as the COVID-19 pandemic demonstrated to the world. Instead, focus on preparing for what you can control in the foreseeable future, that being no more than thirty days out. Budget one month at a time and focus on one area where you can improve your spending plan at a time.

Rather than worrying about every single category you spend money in, find *one* area that you feel you can control and be intentional about that spending over the next month. For example, last month I focused on planning my travel wisely. This month I'm working on my food-spending habits. Next month I'll be focused on budgeting for the holidays.

Every month can—and should—be different. Don't plan for the next month until you feel confident that the current one has been handled well. When you notice yourself thinking beyond the next month, bring yourself back to looking at what you know you can control within the next thirty days.

3. What Is the 80% That I Can Accept As Good Enough?

Remember the power of World Peas, also known as the 80/20 rule, in the previous chapter? Self-proclaimed high achievers have a hard time accepting this advice: When it comes to budgeting, 80% success is good enough!

I have consistently completed a monthly budget since July 2016, and never once has it gone 100% according to plan. In fact, during some of those months, almost *none* of it went according to plan. Yet I still made tons of progress, and you can too—and maybe you can even invest enough to retire early and quit working so hard like I did.

A dead giveaway that your budget isn't accurate is if it looks exactly the same every month. Most people think that budgeting should just include what you need, but you should also allocate money toward variable "want" expenses like holidays, celebrations, and vacations. At the end of every year, I always hear one of my CRUSH Bootcamp members exclaim, "Christmas came out of nowhere," when they could have planned ahead for holiday gifts. What you plan to spend in November and December is probably going to look very different from what you spend in April and May.

A budget is forward-looking, not looking into the past. By treating your budget as a changing plan each month, you'll learn after a few months that a budget doesn't need to be perfect. It's meant to give you peace of mind that you have a plan for the expenses within your control.

Thinking your budget will be exactly right is an unreasonable expectation. When I tell people this, they often respond by audibly letting out a sigh of relief. Budgeting is not an all-or-nothing activity. It's better to do it okay consistently than to do it well without a regular commitment.

4. Did I Limit Regrets to Five Minutes Max?

The biggest mistake I see newbies to budgeting make is rehashing what's already been done: reviewing their past transactions and spending more time beating themselves up than planning for what's ahead. Rather than dissecting individual transactions, look for overall trends in behavior that you can try to shift this month.

For example:

- If you spent more than you planned on clothing last month, commit to using what you already have this month.
- If you didn't invest as much as you hoped for last month, use your budgeting session to put away that goal amount immediately.
- If you ate out at restaurants that in hindsight weren't worth it, make weekly meal prep part of your budgeting routine.

It's helpful to know where you might have encountered unplanned expenses, but limit your review of last month's spending to five minutes tops in your one-hour budgeting session for the upcoming month.

The best way I know to combat an oncoming pity party is to plan your monthly budget meeting with someone you trust. I don't like wasting other people's time with my own insecurities, and I tend to show up more confidently when I am working with someone who I know is awesome too.

If you're in a relationship, budgeting with your partner would be ideal, but that's not always feasible. That's okay. Regularly discussing your budget with someone you've chosen can create positive peer pressure that helps you save more. Consider going outside of your immediate social circle and talk to someone who might have similar financial goals, or whose financial acumen you admire. Find someone you really trust, and don't feel ashamed to share where you might have some challenges. Pick someone as a partner and a sounding board who makes you want to show up like a leader, not just a follower.

You don't necessarily have to discuss every detail of your finances with this person, but you can meet with this person monthly to:

- Share short-term goals you are working on, like paying down debt.
- Get trusted feedback on how you are approaching big purchases.
- Say out loud any worries or concerns and ask for encouragement.
- Hold yourself accountable by sharing your results each month.

You can spend the first five minutes catching up or venting about what went wrong before, but after that, get a move on! You won't resolve your present-day problems by fixating on what can't be undone. In Chapter 7, I'll share with you how you can find a millionaire mentor to hold you accountable.

Caley and Lindsey Grew Their Net Worth Together!

I have two students, Caley and Lindsey, who joined my financial education bootcamp at the same time, and they became budgeting partners. Caley lived in Charlotte while Lindsey lived in New York, and they noticed that they had a lot in common as two thirtysomething single women tackling money goals like paying down credit card debt and learning how to budget well while also trying to grow their careers. They eventually started chatting on the phone once a month to share their progress, vent about money frustrations, and root each other on.

Within two years of coaching with me and with each other, they both paid off all their credit card debt and built three months of Keep Calm Fund savings. Even more amazingly, they both managed to max out their employer 401(k)s—that's over $20,000 a year in investing as millennial women! Even though both of them have since graduated from CRUSH Your Money Goals, we still keep in touch as they enter the next phases of their lives.

5. Have I Practiced for at Least Six Months Before Recalibrating?

Remember, budgeting is a skill, and like most skills, it takes time to master. Even if you've budgeted in the past and are just getting back into the habit, it's unreasonable to expect you'll be great at it from the get-go. Every person I've met who said budgeting "didn't work" only did it for a month or two before they quit. Or they spent so much time fixating on what tool to use or format to follow, they didn't actually learn the process of making financial choices.

My advice? Stick to *one* tool and *one* format for at least three months before you say it doesn't work. Then adjust based on the patterns you find after six months. One month or one try is not enough to say that budgeting isn't effective. And six consecutive months gives you even better data than being on and off throughout the year.

Personally, the winter is my favorite time to practice a new skill like budgeting because the colder months seem to offer fewer distractions of going outside and spending money socializing. Take December, January, and February as your practice months to try a new budgeting routine before you change course. As with joining a gym or other goals, many people commit to New Year's resolutions only to give up by Valentine's Day. Of course, you don't have to wait until December if you're reading this earlier in the year! If you start now and give yourself some practice and time to succeed, come this time next year, you'll know what worked well and what needs improvement.

To make the Cha-Ching Checklist a habit, keep this book in your budgeting spot and bookmark this section so you can review the five questions each month as you start your budgeting meeting.

RICH REFLECTIONS

Have you struggled to stick to a budget in the past, and if so, what barriers have you encountered?

How can you carve out uninterrupted time and energy to focus on your budgeting routine each month?

When do you feel most calm and focused during the month, and how can you leverage this time for budgeting purposes?

What past financial decisions do you keep dwelling on? How is that serving you?

What are three realistic expectations you can keep as you navigate the challenges and successes of budgeting over the next year? For example, if you miss a meeting, you will always make it a point to reschedule.

THE THREE LIFE BUCKETS:
Bye-Bye, Boring Budgets

Now it's time to get down to business and craft your monthly money plan. Remember, feel free to use fun category names, and even add emojis if your software allows it! Here's an example of my budget, where I manage a million dollars' worth of assets every month:

INCOME	
CRUSH Bootcamp	$18,000.00
Easy paychecks	$6,585.78
Risk-free money	$2,500.00
AJ is an influencer	$80.00
SURVIVE	
Home is a vacation	$2,622.00
Food is fuel	$1,200.00
Too much screen time	$300.00
Keeping it lit	$200.00
Car	$300.00
State Farm renters' renewal	$70.00
REVIVE	
Family birthdays	$600.00
Massage health	$300.00
Hip-hop foundations	$200.00
Need my yoga nidra	$80.00

STRIVE	
Business investments	$5,000.00
Save up for next home	$3,358.78
Client bookkeeping	$2,400.00
Team office	$1,350.00
Taxes + bookkeeping	$485.00
Transaction fees	$300.00
Subscriptions	$500.00
Keep Calm Fund	$0.00
Trips	$4,000.00
1Q est. tax payment	$3,900.00

And guess what? You can set up something like this too, no matter your income level. And trust me, we're going to have some fun with this. Surprisingly, it'll take less than an hour a month to maintain once you've got it set up. Yes, setting up this monthly money plan will take some up-front time and effort, like all good things do. But think of it as an investment in your financial future. Once you've got this habit in place, it's going to serve you for life, whether you're making $30,000 or $300,000 a year—or even more! I'm rooting for your success here, truly.

Embrace the Three Buckets

When I first started to budget, I had more than forty different line items on my list to capture anything and everything I might spend money on in a given month. Keeping track of that many things got tedious very quickly, and I found it hard to notice any significant patterns in my spending that would help me save more money.

Forget the overwhelming minutiae and the drudgery of having dozens of line items on your budget to keep track of, because that's likely what bored you to tears in the past. My advice is to instead divide your budget into three main buckets: Survive, Revive, and Strive. *Survive* and *revive* are derivatives of the Latin word *vivere*, meaning "to live." (I took two years of Latin in high school to supposedly get better SAT scores, but I digress.)

Each of these buckets is all about living your best life, tailored to your unique preferences and goals. I like to think of my budget as a living, breathing representation of who I am and who I want to be.

 The Three Buckets Work

I converted Greta into a budgeting believer. She joined my CRUSH Bootcamp after a recommendation from her sister, who came through my bootcamp. Greta said, "I love the simplicity of the three buckets. Survive is relatively fixed every month (with some exceptions, of course!), so then it becomes about planning for Strive and remembering to allocate for Revive. So far it's been a good reminder to spend some money on us and things we like to do."

Philosophically, I believe that someone should be able to look at your budget and know exactly what kind of person you are and what matters to you most. If that's not the case, you're not only doing a budget wrong in my opinion, you're also highly unlikely to stick to it. Let's dive into each of these buckets in detail.

Your Budget Starts with "Survive"

Survive covers the five essentials—housing, utilities, food, transportation, and health. These are nonnegotiables, and we're not dwelling on them because, well, life's about more than just surviving. You may recognize these same five items from the Cash Flow Cushion habit because they are exactly that—the basic bills you will likely pay regardless of whether or not you have income. In a bit more detail, this bucket includes the following five line items:

- Mortgage or rent and other housing expenses such as taxes and insurance
- Utilities including your phone, Internet, and other modern-day services
- Food expenses, no matter if you buy groceries, eat at restaurants, or order delivery
- Transportation expenses including your car payments, gas, parking, and commuting expenses
- Health expenses such as household supplies, personal hygiene, and medical expenses

This bucket should include expenses for everyone in your home, including your pets. They say dogs are the new kids, right? I also am a big advocate of mental health care, and so I believe any related expenses such as therapy should also be included in your Survive bucket under health.

FEWER LINE ITEMS MEANS MAKING SMARTER CHOICES

Once I condensed my budget into these three categories, I noticed some significant patterns indicating where I could improve my financial decisions:

- My debt payments were taking up a higher percentage of our monthly income than I expected.
- We could free up more money toward vacations as long as we planned ahead.
- If we tried to work toward making Strive a bigger portion of our monthly budget, we could speed up our retirement plan by decades.

By grouping line items together underneath these three larger categories, I felt less overwhelmed. It also gave me more flexibility to exchange spending among different items within each category.

"Revive" Makes Room for Guilt-Free Spending

When I first started researching how to budget to pay off my student loans, a lot of the personal finance guides advocated for first paying for essentials (in other words, the items in your Survive bucket), then allocating the rest to pay down your debt. I tried that approach myself for a few months, and wow, that was totally soul sucking and absolutely no fun! Even more importantly, I started to feel like giving up on budgeting altogether because I was tired of feeling deprived.

I decided I needed to have at least *some* portion of my budget going toward enjoying my life and pursuing peace. Revive is where you can indulge your desires guilt-free. Vacations, hobbies, treats—it's all fair game. No shame here, folks. This is where your budget really starts to look different from everyone else's, and it should! You're a unique human being, after all.

In the Revive bucket for AJ and me today, you'll find monthly massages, trips to see my extended family, yoga, dance classes, and fashion. We used to feel bad about those things, but what's the point of having money if you don't enjoy spending it?

My CRUSH Bootcamp members are often surprised to find Revive as a necessary part of their budgets, because those paying down debt assume that they aren't allowed to have any fun. But I learned that having a meaningful Revive budget can actually help you spend less money overall, because you're intentional about what you spend. The Revive bucket helps you focus on what genuinely makes you happy or helps you calm down.

"Strive" Is How You Achieve Financial Freedom

The Strive bucket is all about building wealth. It's also what's always overlooked in other budgeting templates I've seen. The vast majority focus on Survive, and a few make room for Revive, but very little attention goes to Strive.

This bucket includes money you're saving, investing, and using to pay down debts—anything that moves the needle on growing your overall net worth.

For example, it can include:

- Money you're saving toward your Keep Calm Fund and Cash Flow Cushion
- Debts you're paying off, including extra payments toward credit cards, personal loans, student loans, car payments, and mortgages
- Investments you're making in your retirement accounts, brokerage accounts, or property
- Education you're paying for, such as coaching, courses, and certificates that can help you increase your income
- Business expenses that help you grow your revenue or increase your efficiency

The word "strive" means "to make great efforts to achieve or obtain something," and so it makes sense that this category should get most of your attention if you want to reach financial freedom.

Try It Out Before You Count It Out!

If you've felt discouraged by your budget in the past, the Three Life Buckets can help motivate you. No more overcomplicating things! It does take some time getting used to a new skill, so give yourself six months to get consistent with budgeting per our Cha-Ching Checklist (see how these habits are starting to stack?). Even if you don't get it perfect every month, you'll make more progress in your financial goals if you at least make a plan with good intentions.

For real-life examples and step-by-step tutorials on how to budget using the Three Life Buckets, head to CRUSHYourMoneyGoals.com. You'll find live and recorded trainings in which I personally walk you through your first budget in this format. Pairing the Three Life Buckets with the next habit will help you focus on what truly matters: managing your money with purpose—and enjoying the journey along the way.

RICH REFLECTIONS

What mindset shifts are necessary for you to value budgeting as a tool for achieving financial freedom?

How does the concept of the Three Life Buckets resonate with your financial goals and aspirations for achieving freedom?

How do you feel about the idea of dedicating a portion of your budget to Revive—personal enjoyment and fulfillment?

What have you been using as Revive but isn't really reviving you anymore? What should you replace it with?

What is one major barrier you anticipate as you implement the Three Life Buckets, and how do you plan to overcome it?

THE ZERO-HERO STRATEGY:
Allocate Every Dollar

Is all your income accounted for when you do your budget at the beginning of the month? People often plan for the expenses they know they have, thinking they'll send any funds left over at the end of the month to their bigger money goals, like paying off debt or adding to savings.

I think you already know where I'm going with this. The intention is great, but when you take that approach, you likely won't have any funds left over. Instead I advocate for what's referred to as a zero-based budget, and it works well because it sets the intention for all the money you expect to have available. I refer to it as the Zero-Hero Strategy because this habit made my debt payoff plan clear, allowing me to pay off $72,000 of student loans in less than a year. I totally feel like a hero whenever I get my budget down to zero—it's so satisfying!

Is Leftover Money *Really* a Good Thing?

Let's address the elephant in the room: The notion that leftover money in your budget is somehow a good thing is not true. I'll be honest—I had a really hard time accepting this because my dad told me that having extra money was something to aim for. Sure, it's tempting to envision those extra dollars piling up in your savings account or chipping away at your debt. But here's the kicker—by leaving money unallocated, you're missing out on the chance to intentionally plan how to maximize every cent and supercharge toward financial freedom faster.

Rather than waiting for possible leftovers, allocate *all* the money you have coming in, including the amount you want to put toward your bigger line items, before the month even starts. This concept goes against the grain of traditional thinking—instead of being a positive thing, leftover money is seen as a missed opportunity and zero is your ultimate destination in your monthly budgeting meeting. You read that right. Zero, as in allocating every last cent of your income, isn't just acceptable; it's the key to feeling like a hero about your money plan.

YOU DON'T HAVE TO LIKE THE MESSENGER TO LIKE THE MESSAGE

Personal finance personality Dave Ramsey is a vocal advocate of the zero-based budgeting approach. His style of messaging can feel polarizing or unrelatable for some. But he's actually not the one who invented the concept. Zero-based budgeting was developed in the 1970s by Pete Pyhrr, an employee at Texas Instruments. As an accounting manager, his original goal was to help companies reduce expenses and promote financial responsibility, where the budget was started from scratch, or a "zero base," each year.

Countless success stories attest to the transformative power of this method, from paying off massive debts to achieving long-held financial aspirations. Female financial influencers I admire who advocate for this approach with an encouraging and uplifting message include Stefanie Gonzales of Women's Wealth Effect; Carmen A. Perez, founder of Use Much and Make Real Cents; and lawyer-turned-financial-author Cindy Zuniga-Sanchez. If you've dismissed the concept because of a particular messenger, find other financial influences that resonate with you more. Don't let one messenger ruin a good idea for you!

Perhaps the most compelling reason I am downright obsessed with being a Zero Hero is having more flexibility. Regardless of your income level or financial situation, this strategy can be tailored to fit your needs and unique circumstances. Whether you're a recent graduate saddled with student loans or a seasoned professional planning for retirement, the Zero-Hero Strategy offers a simpler road map to financial freedom.

Give Every Dollar a Meaningful Place

So, how do you implement the Zero-Hero Strategy in your own life? First, embrace the idea that every dollar has a purpose. Begin by listing all your sources of income, even if they're small amounts. For example, our rental building pays AJ $20 in credit toward our rent for posting a picture every Wednesday. Even if it's only $80 a month, we still put it in our budget!

Allocating each dollar of income all the way down to zero isn't just a task —it's a state of mind, a symbol of financial empowerment, and a pathway to a brighter financial future.

The habit of proactively assigning every dollar of your income to a specific expense before the month even begins not only ensures every dollar has a job. The power of this habit lies in its extreme intentionality. By deliberately assigning each dollar to a purpose, you eliminate ambiguity and gain clarity on exactly where your money is going. This level of precision is what sets your financial-goal achievements apart from the average person's, whether you're paying off debt, investing for retirement, or saving for a dream vacation.

DITCH THE SPREADSHEETS AND OPT FOR AN ONLINE APP

There are tons of budgeting apps out there, and the way I construct my budget means it can be done in Excel or using pen and paper with a good old-fashioned calculator. But the downside to both those options is that it's hard to see trends across time, and I find most clients who use Excel spend way more time fiddling with making the spreadsheet formulas than actually making financial choices.

Instead, I highly recommend you keep your budget online so you can track your progress over not just months, but years. The first option I have found to be effective is an online app called EveryDollar. It's free, it's user-friendly, and yes, it's a Dave Ramsey product. But don't worry, I'm not here to push his agenda. I've just found it to be the simplest option out there. And for many of my CRUSH Bootcamp members who don't have much disposable income, the free option works great. I used the tool for seven years and never needed the paid version.

The second option I recommend is a product called Monarch Money, which charges a monthly fee. It's the tool I personally use because it combines both what I need for budgeting as well as for tracking my net worth. One of the upsides of Monarch Money is you are able to share your budget with household members and potentially a financial coach like myself without having to share your passwords. It's also fun because there are a lot of emojis to use!

Let me be crystal clear—achieving zero isn't about depriving yourself or living on a boring budget. On the contrary, it's about prioritizing your spending based on what truly matters to you. By aligning the Three Life Buckets with the habit of making zero your budgeting goal every month, you are even more empowered to align your spending with your true values.

Remember These Three Things As You Strategize to Get to Zero

Let me lay down three truth bombs to make sure you're in the right frame of mind to use the Zero-Hero Strategy well.

1. First off, you're normal. This is my nice way of saying you're not that special. Seriously, with nearly 350 million people in America alone, your financial situation is likely more typical than you think. So, before you assume that your unique circumstances are the root of your budgeting woes, trust me, this approach will work for you. I've seen it work across hundreds of CRUSH Bootcamp members, many of whom at first thought it wouldn't work for them.
2. Secondly, you don't have millions of dollars or endless hours to waste on reinventing budgeting tools. There are plenty of tools out there that have been developed by teams with serious resources behind them. Leverage that expertise rather than trying to DIY your way through with a spreadsheet or pen and paper. The point of budgeting is to make choices, not track transactions.

   Now, I know some of you might be skeptical. You've tried various tools and apps, maybe even the ones I've mentioned. But here's the deal: If budgeting hasn't worked for you in the past—I am going to break it to you kindly—it's probably not the tool's fault; it's likely yours. Tools are only as good as your ability to use them well and consistently. But don't be hard on yourself. Remember you need to practice before you get good!
3. Lastly, let's not confuse activity with achievement. Many new CRUSH Bootcamp members get hung up on this concept because they were conditioned to believe that tracking every penny is what makes budgeting

valuable. Recording those expenses would be similar to writing down the times you plan to brush your teeth or take a shower—it's just checking things off a list, and it creates extra administrative work but not a change in behavior.

Do you think millionaires spend their time tracking every little penny? No, they plan for the life they want, not just the life they already have. You might feel the urge to track your expenses for the first three months after starting a new budget if you really have no idea how much you spend. But after that period, you start to get a sense of where you need to plan and where you can automate paying expenses.

This budgeting approach isn't just about reaching zero—it's about embracing the power of intentionality, prioritizing your financial freedom, and taking control of your money like never before. Why settle for leftovers when you can have it all? Embrace this new skill and watch as your financial dreams become a reality. Zero has never looked so zen.

RICH REFLECTIONS

What lessons have you learned from previous budgeting attempts, and how do you plan to apply them to your zero-based budgeting approach?

How do you feel about the idea of giving every dollar a job within your budget, and how do you plan to manage any feelings of restriction or deprivation that may arise?

What are some areas where you typically overspend or underspend, and how do you plan to address those tendencies within your Zero-Hero budget?

What inspires you about the Zero-Hero budgeting approach, and how do you envision it helping you achieve your financial goals?

If you don't hit zero next month, what will be your course of action to try to hit zero the following month? What will you tell yourself to stay encouraged? Write it on a sticky note.

THE FINANCIAL INDEPENDENCE FORMULA:
Calculate How Much Money You Need to Retire

I'll be honest with you. The idea of retirement hasn't always really resonated with me as a motivation to get moving on my finances. I started nerding out on personal finance in my early thirties, so retirement wasn't anywhere on my list of priorities. That's why I now recommend that you figure out how much money you need to retire as soon as you can, so that you're not caught by surprise the way many baby boomers are now.

As I mentioned earlier, my MBA program precipitated my interest, or rather panic, in personal finance when I finally logged in and found that I had over $72,000 in student loans accruing interest daily. With the average student loan balance at $28,950 owed per borrower (as of June 2024), financial independence may feel even more far-fetched if you are saddled with student loans and other types of debt like I was.

I had a couple of MBA classmates who were praised for being committed, ideal students: a pregnant classmate still taking her final exam while in the early stages of labor, and a poster child CEO who did not miss his board meeting even though he collapsed from a health condition. I saw what was considered "successful" as putting one's health and family behind one's ambition, and that never felt good to me.

On the other side of the spectrum, you may have met wealthier people who, despite having enough to retire, work even harder. I have an uncle who became financially successful by growing and maintaining a tax-accounting business for decades, such that he could afford a luxury condo in New York City and a second home in the Philippines. He was generous enough to contribute money into my college savings ever since I was a kid. I used that money to go for a college semester abroad in London, when my parents couldn't afford to pay for it.

He's been generous with his money, but the last time I went to visit him, he was still doing taxes in his business at over eighty years old—he's never actually retired. It's not because he needs the money. He said it's to keep his brain active.

I asked him what else he liked to do that could keep his brain active: learn a new language, play games, read more books perhaps? He couldn't think of anything, until I showed him how he could sing karaoke on his television using YouTube and a handheld microphone. That day he started singing Frank Sinatra, and it was the first time I'd seen him sing in years! Sometimes, we just need to be reminded of the things we used to love.

The Definition of Retirement Is Personal

As I mentioned earlier, the idea of retiring early inspired me to reach beyond just becoming debt-free and become truly financially free. And I did just that—my husband and I moved from the city to the mountains for two years and did a lot of relaxing to see if retiring early was what it was chalked up to be. We read books, we hiked, we became hipster millennials and started collecting records and vintage clothes. When the world opened up again after the COVID-19 pandemic, we traveled to Portugal, South Korea, and France, and all across the US.

But something unexpected happened that shook me to my core. I realized that I actually wanted to keep working! I could afford to not work for a while, but I still found myself excited to coach new CRUSH Bootcamp members, practice my journalism skills, and try my hand at paid speaking. It turned out that work itself wasn't the problem. It was the fact that for over a decade I had done work that didn't excite me and didn't align with my real interests and talents.

Prevailing thoughts about retirement are always changing. Decades ago, most middle- and upper-class white Americans were all but guaranteed a retirement, many through pension funds. Over the years, trends such as "financial independence, retire early" (FIRE) have come and gone—for many, retiring early is simply not an option. For the CRUSH Bootcamp, I've decided to focus solely on financial independence, or having enough money to live without working if you choose to. I heard about this concept from several other personal finance nerds, such as Jill Schlesinger, and I really love it for myself and for my CRUSH Bootcamp members because it tosses out the concept of traditional retirement. It opens up the idea that if you reach your financial independence goal, you can choose whatever it is you want to do—whether it's to keep working, spend more time with family, travel, or indulge in completely new interests.

> ### THE FINANCIAL INDEPENDENCE MOVEMENT
>
> Vicki Robin and Joe Dominguez, who authored the book *Your Money or Your Life* in 1992, promoted spending retirement years enjoying hobbies, family, and friends instead of working into your sixties. They called this plan the financial independence movement—and its principles contributed to the foundations of the CRUSH Bootcamp.

Calculate Your Financial Independence Number

There is an actual way to calculate how much money you need to become financially free. There is a simple formula that can help you find your financial independence number and save money more strategically starting today. Though the math isn't hard, the end number may feel overwhelming—but hang on! It won't be as bad as you think.

According to traditional retirement formulas, you need to have 25 times your annual expenses in investments. This formula also assumes that you will withdraw 4% of your retirement fund each year once you stop working. The general idea is that while you do withdraw your living expenses, the invested amount is simultaneously replenishing that money through compound interest, growth in value, or dividends.

Does that sound a little scary to you? Are you thinking, *What in the world, Bernadette?! I came here to learn some simple money habits and now you're telling me I have to have 25 times my annual expenses? Bye, girl, bye! This is too overwhelming!*

Good. Being overwhelmed means you are entering unfamiliar territory. I warned you this would be a challenge! Remind yourself you're up for at least giving it a try!

We touched on this in broad terms earlier in the book, but now it's time to calculate this more specifically. I recommend first adding up the total monthly expenses in your Survive bucket.

As a reminder, these five basic budgeting lines are:

- Housing, consisting of either your rent or mortgage and associated costs such as taxes and insurance
- Utilities, such as your electricity, cell phone bill, and Internet
- Food, including what you eat beyond groceries
- Transportation, including car payment, insurance, gas, and parking
- Health, including household items you need to stay healthy, like shampoo and cleaning supplies, as well as health expenses for your medical and wellness needs

After you calculate your Survive total on a monthly basis, you can multiply by 12 to get your annual amount. Then you can multiply by 25 to get what you would need in order to become financially independent. For example, if your monthly Survive bucket is $4,000, your target financial independence number would be $4,000 × 12 × 25 to equal $1,200,000.

This number assumes that you only withdraw 4% of the total each year. Since the investments are also replenishing through compound interest, growing in value or dividends, you are unlikely to run out of money in your lifetime. This formula is backed by research, such as the "Trinity study," which was landmark research in personal finance that analyzed the sustainability of retirement portfolios. Conducted by professors at Trinity University in 1998, it concluded that an investment portfolio with at least 50% stocks had a high success rate of lasting 30 years with a 4% annual withdrawal rate. This study forms the basis for the "4% rule," a guideline still used by many financial advisors to determine a safe withdrawal rate from your retirement savings. If that feels confusing, don't worry. What you need to understand is the rule isn't perfect, but it's served as a guideline and starting point for planning retirement.

How You Choose to React to Your Number Can Improve Your Odds

When teaching this formula to my financial education students, I typically get one of three responses. The first is that people immediately assume a number of 25 times their yearly expenses is impossible to reach. This is understandable because even when you have relatively low monthly expenses, it's likely your financial independence number will be more than $1 million. It's a hard pill to swallow, hearing that you need to be a millionaire to afford a basic standard of living in the United States.

The second response is that people start dissecting the 4% rule and its flaws and then go into a spiral of how it doesn't make sense in our day and age thanks to inflation, interest rates, the government, the economy, or any other external factor over which individuals have no influence. These learners typically spend more time overanalyzing than executing and find themselves getting frustrated by their lack of momentum.

But my favorite response is the third one, where learners go into a short shock moment, process their feelings about the difficulty of achieving their number, but then start asking questions on how they can inch their way closer to it. These learners feel hopeful that for the first time, they have a target to aim for rather than "as much money as possible." They find inspiration in the knowing versus not.

Feel Your Feelings about the Number

Here are some real-life reactions I've gotten from my CRUSH Bootcamp during live learning sessions:

- "That's a big number! I guess I'm doomed."
- "I feel so discouraged."
- "I don't even spend that much; how is this even possible?"

These reactions are totally understandable. But don't despair—you *can* do this. I think of pursuing financial independence like competing in the Olympics. Imagine if every athlete said, "I'm probably not going to win the gold medal, so why bother?" There would be no Olympics, and we wouldn't get to witness some of the most amazing examples of human achievement.

And herein lies the truth about financial independence: There might be a lot of things working against you, but you cannot control those things. You can't control the government. You can't control inflation. You can't control the stock market. You can't control interest rates. You can't control other people, even the ones close to you (nor should you).

The only things you can control are your own habits—and that's why this book will focus on those topics. Let's say you in fact never reach this financial independence number. Would you still be better off if you achieved 50% of it? What if you achieved even just 10% of it? Giving up before you even start is a surefire path to failure, so feel your feelings, and let's keep moving!

Erin Is the Rich Auntie She Dreamed of Being

Erin is a lifelong Chicagoan and the oldest of three sisters. She lost her mother to breast cancer as a young adult and moved back home to help take care of her youngest sister, who was born when Erin was a senior in high school. By keeping her promise to her mom, Erin learned what it was like to be a parent and has a very close relationship with her sisters.

"The biggest change I've seen is thinking about money in terms of net worth. Since I've focused on net worth, I've paid off my credit card debt and I'm tackling my student loans. Before, I was passive about money. I worried about not having enough but I never sat down and spent time with my money to make it work for me." Make no mistake, Erin's money is working hard. She has increased her net worth by more than $100,000 and will be debt-free this year!

By working the CRUSH system, Erin is dreaming big. And by big, I mean early retirement. "Bernadette helped me figure out my retirement number. It's not as daunting as I initially thought. I once thought that I needed to work until sixty-five because I needed a pension to retire, and now I plan to retire from my nine-to-five while I'm still young-ish. I'm still pinching myself. This doesn't feel real. I'm amazed that she has gotten me to love using an app to develop a monthly budget. I am both more organized and less stressed about money. I enjoy tracking my net worth and making strategic decisions for my money instead of just spending or not spending and hoping for the best."

Erin now sees the big picture when it comes to money and wants to pay it forward to the young people in her life. "I want to train my nieces, nephews, great-nieces, and great-nephews to view money the way that I now do as a result of my time with Bernadette. This is the best inheritance I could leave for them."

Start by Paying Off Debt and Streamlining Expenses

To kick-start my own early-retirement plan, I resolved to maintain a more essentialist lifestyle and find ways to streamline those five basic survival expenses by paying off debts like car loans and credit card balances. I even went so far as to pay off my mortgage once I realized that taking off that monthly bill of about $2,000 could lower my overall financial independence number by a whopping $600,000. Before you dismiss the idea of investing 25 times your expenses, consider what impact investing even 10% of your total freedom number could have on your quality of life.

You may not be able to leave your career, but recalculating your financial independence number at least once a year using this investing formula will help you stay on track. When you make a habit of calculating this number annually based on your most up-to-date Survive number, it means you can root your plan in facts, not feeling. Resolving to take small steps and at least attempting to move toward investing your freedom number can move you years or even decades closer to independence.

RICH REFLECTIONS

Have you ever felt pressured to prove your worth through excessive work? How has that influenced your financial goals?

Did any specific events or realizations prompt you to become more interested in getting good with money, and if so, how did they impact your approach to managing money?

Consider your initial reaction to your financial independence number. Did you feel overwhelmed, skeptical, or motivated when learning about your number? How do you plan to address these feelings moving forward?

How can you shift from overanalyzing external factors to focusing on actionable steps you can take to improve your financial situation and move closer to your number?

How do you envision your life once you achieve financial freedom, and what endeavors or experiences are you most looking forward to?

5 Understand Your (Net) Worth

Now that you've read about budgeting habits in Chapter 4—including the Cha-Ching Checklist, the Three Life Buckets, and the Zero-Hero Strategy—it's time to put them into practice with one main goal: to understand and grow your net worth toward achieving faster financial independence. The habits in this step of the CRUSH plan will help you assess everything you own and everything you owe so that you have a comprehensive picture of your financial standing.

When you are pursuing financial independence, your asset allocations will differ from what one might see in more traditional financial frameworks. Many proponents of financial independence aim toward more aggressive savings rates to accelerate the journey. A key principle of reaching financial independence is to maximize your savings rate, often targeting up to 70% of your income. This means allocating the majority of your budget toward savings, investments, and paying down debt.

This approach certainly will speed up your wealth accumulation. Since the goal is to minimize expenses and get to financial independence as fast as possible, people this strict often focus on getting their Survive buckets down to the absolute bare essentials. This often involves adopting a super-minimalist lifestyle—downsizing housing, living with roommates or family members, minimizing transportation expenses, or adhering to a strict food budget.

While that's certainly one way to approach it, in this chapter I want to help you focus on how to better understand your net worth and how you can grow it while still living your life and having fun if going super minimalist feels daunting or is just not your jam.

As always, these habits are ones that I've personally employed to reach my financial independence goals and ones I encourage you to grow over time, even though they might sometimes feel hard. I chose these five habits because they cover topics that I've seen CRUSH Bootcamp members have the most challenges with—largely because of the societal expectations so many of us feel pressured to fall in line with in a modern world. But I learned that it pays (literally) to be contrarian to what the patriarchy dictates! Here are the five net worth habits that can grow your wealth faster than just working hard.

THE BUCKETS BREAKDOWN:
Save and Invest 50% of Your Income

In the Three Life Buckets habit in Chapter 4, you learned how to divvy up your expenses into three categories: Survive, Revive, and Strive. Here's a reminder of what falls into each of your three budgeting buckets:

- **Survive**—basic necessities, including housing, utilities, food, transportation, and health
- **Revive**—current expenses that aren't necessary but make life worth living for you, like vacations, clothing, entertainment, and hobbies
- **Strive**—anything that helps you grow your overall net worth, like your Keep Calm Fund, your Cash Flow Cushion, debt payments, investing, and expenses for a business you own

The critical part we haven't discussed yet is how much to allocate to each bucket. There are varying opinions on what the right proportions are when it comes to budgeting. Here are some of the most common examples:

- **50/30/20 rule:** Proposed by Elizabeth Warren and Amelia Warren Tyagi in the book *All Your Worth*, this rule suggests allocating 50% of your income toward needs, 30% toward wants, and 20% toward savings and debt repayment.
- **70/20/10 rule:** With this rule, 70% of income is allocated to needs, 20% to savings and debt repayment, and 10% to donations.
- **60/20/20 rule:** Similar to the 50/30/20 rule, this guideline suggests 60% of income toward needs (which often includes debt payments); 20% toward savings, investments, and debt repayment; and 20% toward wants.

Perhaps you have followed one of these before. Having a framework to follow is definitely better than not having one at all, so kudos to you if you've already been on this path! The commonality across all these examples is that the bulk of your income is weighted toward your current needs.

While that's a great starting point to ensure you are not spending outside of what you can afford, it keeps you within the parameters of traditional financial planning—thus also keeping you at a normal retirement age at best.

The CRUSH Method: 50% Strive/25% Survive/25% Revive

Instead of these options, I recommend a budget breakdown of 50/25/25 with the target of 50% eventually allocated toward growing your net worth (Strive) and the other half split between what you need in the present (Survive) and what you want in the present (Revive). I fully recognize that this is not an easy framework to follow, and that's okay. Financial freedom is hard to attain, but it's not impossible! This allocation of your income helps you reach financial freedom faster because most people are living and acting paycheck to paycheck, remember? Aiming to eventually save and invest 50% of your income toward your future means that you are buying years of your future freedom now.

A First Step: 25% Strive/50% Survive/25% Revive

If 50/25/25 won't work for you at the moment, start with the same ratios but flipped: 50% toward Survive and the other half split between Revive and Strive. This step allows you to diagnose whether you are living within your means or if you have an income issue. If your Survive bucket is exceeding 50% of your income, it more often signals an income shortage than it signals someone with irresponsible spending habits.

Many of my CRUSH Bootcamp members sighed with relief when they heard this, because they couldn't understand how to cut any more when other experts told them they were spending too much. If you've truly cut everything you can in Survive and are still exceeding 50% of your budget, your focus needs to be on growing your income more than cutting expenses.

The reason I found this framework to be more effective is that it is relatively easy math for people to calculate in their heads. You essentially split your income in half, then split the other half in half, and you have your three buckets. The philosophical way I like to think about this approach is how you're honoring yourself. Spending 50% of your budget on Survive to start off with is honoring your current needs. The other half is split between living a happy life in the present (Revive) and living a happy life in the future (Strive). It also helps clarify why you need to pay down debt. Debt, to me, represents your past, and investments represent your future. It's hard to keep striving if you're weighed down by your past, so it's best to pay down your debts first so you can then focus your efforts toward your future goals in the Strive bucket. Once you've stabilized your budget to consistently meet the 25% Strive/50% Survive/25% Revive ratio for at least six months, then you can start moving toward flipping the ratios to weigh more toward Strive than Survive.

The other reason I find this framework to be more effective than the others is because that Revive bucket target stays at 25% regardless of where you are in your journey. That's because so many other "get rich" experts will tell you that the answer is to have no fun and work to the bone. But I learned from personal experience that you will not only burn out, but you'll hate budgeting so much that you'll just abandon it altogether. Keeping a healthy portion of your budget allocated toward enjoying your life now will help you stay on the journey longer because you won't feel so deprived.

Being Too Extreme Can Lead to Guilt, Even When You Can Finally Afford It

You may be surprised to hear this, but I don't advocate putting more than 50% of your budget toward Strive for a prolonged amount of time unless you are a high earner ($200,000 or more in annual income). For many of us, it takes a lot of planning just to get to that 50% Strive target, especially with so many Americans saddled with consumer debt that previous generations didn't have.

According to a 2023 CNBC Financial Confidence Survey, 70% of Americans reported feeling stress about their personal finances, and 52% said their financial stress had increased since before the COVID-19 pandemic. AJ and I finished paying off all our debt in 2019 largely because we were highly aggressive on our Strive goals. This greatly helped our mental health during the pandemic, while many of our peers were concerned about paying their bills.

But there was a trade-off that I didn't expect. Even when we reached our financial independence number, I still felt guilty for spending on Revive items like travel, live concerts, and clothing—even though they were well within our means and I had planned for them in advance. I witnessed this as well with my parents-in-law, who recently paid off all their debt including their mortgage. Despite having saved up enough for retirement after living rather frugally for decades, and despite having relatively low expenses, they are still worried they will run out of money.

While I am, and always will be, a huge proponent of pursuing financial freedom, I wish I had loosened up my budget a bit more while I was still in the process. Now that I teach financial education to the CRUSH Bootcamp, I encourage them to spend around 25% of their budget on Revive versus delaying recreational spending for too long. With this proportion as a habit, you can learn a healthier balance between saving for the future and spending in the present.

In the upcoming chapters, I'll share more specific strategies on how you can creatively achieve this targeted budget breakdown of 50/25/25 without having to take it to the extremes of frugality.

RICH REFLECTIONS

How does having a 50/25/25 target for your three buckets simplify your decision-making? How will it help you keep focused month to month?

Evaluate your spending patterns in the Survive category. Are there any areas where you could potentially reduce expenses to allocate more toward Strive and Revive?

Reflect on the progress you've made in your financial journey so far. Celebrate your achievements in each of the three buckets the way you would support your best friend.

Will allocating 25% toward Revive be easy or hard for you? What are you looking forward to in your Revive budget?

What's one big move you can make to start flipping the targets toward 50% in Strive? How can you cultivate a mindset of growth and wealth accumulation within the Strive category?

THE VESTED VEHICLE:
Save Face and Car Costs

For most people, the cost to finance their car is likely their largest monthly expense outside of their housing expenses. After all, at least one car is a necessity for most families in the United States. I felt it was important to include a habit specifically around car buying and maintenance because I've witnessed via my CRUSH Bootcamp members how that one purchase decision can materially make or break a person's financial plan.

In early 2024, drivers were spending over $700 a month for new cars and $500 for used ones, with insurance costing an average of $2,014 per year, according to Bankrate. And despite the technological advances, it doesn't feel like car prices will ever go down. In late 2023, new cars cost an average of $48,247, while used cars averaged $26,533, according to Cox Automotive data.

In simple terms, if you are "vested" in a certain investment asset, it means that you have full ownership and control over it. However, according to a survey of over one thousand Americans conducted by *GOBankingRates*, 40% stated that they had a monthly car payment and therefore did not own their cars outright. So, let's discuss the strategies around the habit I like to call the Vested Vehicle and how you can drive for freedom!

Your Car Expenses Need to Be under 15% of Your Budget

Costs related to your car fall in the Survive bucket as part of your transportation costs. I agree with the general consensus that to be within your means, your car payments should not exceed 10 to 15% of your net income. You can use a car loan calculator to figure out where you stand. I've seen past CRUSH members whose monthly car payments crossed over $1,000 a month, constituting way more than the recommended ratio.

There are a lot of reasons that car payments can balloon to that amount. For example, people sometimes purchase cars beyond their budgets, pay extra in interest due to their credit scores, or agree to longer-than-necessary loan terms. Unfortunately, the cost of poor purchase decisions like that can set you back years in reaching any sort of stability, let alone financial independence. And that's not including the insurance, parking, and maintenance costs we need to consider!

Remember our budgeting breakdown? If your total Survive percentage to start off with is 50% and your car is taking up 15% of it, that only leaves 35% for your other necessities like housing, utilities, food, and health expenses. If you're working on a more aggressive financial independence plan, then your Survive percentage will be closer to 25% of your net income, and 15% would be more than half of that. This is why it's super helpful to have a paid-off car if you can prioritize that in your budget—money that would be going toward interest payments on your loan could be going toward investing in your future instead.

Don't Wait Until the Wheels Fall Off

While the sentiment is great—save as much money as possible by driving your car to the ground—at some point, you start trading savings for safety. Typically, eight to ten years is a safe amount of time to be driving a car if it's new, and if you're buying a used car that's three to five years old, then driving it for five to seven years makes sense. The average length of car ownership is around 12.5 years, which is definitely doable for a well-made vehicle. I teach my CRUSH Bootcamp to assume that they will need to buy a new car every ten years and to start saving for their next car as soon as four years earlier to when they expect to need it.

Waiting until you absolutely need to buy your next car is not a great idea for a couple of reasons. First, an old car puts you in a stressful situation, because it will need more repairs and take up time and money as you deal with those maintenance issues. Second, it puts you in a terrible negotiating position when you go to purchase a new car, because you've backed yourself into the corner of *needing* the car now rather than being able to wait until the right car and deal come along. I often remind my CRUSH Bootcamp that it's not a matter of *if* they'll need a new car; it's a matter of *when*. It's a much better idea to plan for the next purchase so it is not as stressful a process when the time finally arrives.

IS LEASING A BAD IDEA?

While overall I advocate for buying your car outright so you are fully vested in it, leasing may make sense based on your financial situation. Lease payments are typically lower than loan payments for the same vehicle, as you're only paying for the depreciation of the car over the lease term rather than the full purchase price. Leasing also often requires a lower down payment or sometimes no down payment at all, making it more affordable to acquire a new car without a large initial investment.

Leasing can also be less of a hassle for busy people. Leasing allows you to drive a new car with the latest features and technology every few years, without the inconvenience of selling or trading in an older vehicle. Leased vehicles are usually covered by the manufacturer's warranty for the length of the term. This can reduce your out-of-pocket expenses for repairs and maintenance, and you may encounter fewer maintenance issues and expenses compared to owning an older vehicle. A lease payment may make sense for you in the short term, but of course, having no car payment at all will help you reach financial independence faster.

Buy Your Car Outright versus Financing It

One of the biggest reasons AJ and I were able to reach financial freedom faster is that we have never financed a car in the fourteen years we've been together. I understand that buying your first or next car outright might be a stretch for you, especially if you've never prioritized that in the past. You may need to finance your first car, or your next car, but it doesn't need to become a habit to finance cars for the rest of your life if you plan ahead.

Consider making the next car that you will inevitably need to purchase a priority as part of your financial independence plan. For example, if you're planning to buy an average used car for $28,000 roughly four years from today, then aim for a goal of saving $7,000 a year or about $584 a month to put toward that future car purchase. I recommend that my clients save this money alongside their Keep Calm Fund in a high-yield savings account so that it can earn a bit of interest while they build up their funds.

Quinn Is Winning with a Paid-Off Car!

Quinn is one of my original CRUSH Bootcamp members, and she has become a friend I'm proud to know. She started by paying off the $16,000 balance of her car in 2020 in just three months. "I had a goal to pay it off by the end of the first quarter of 2021, but realized I could do it sooner than I had planned. Owning my car outright gives me so much satisfaction, and now I can put the monthly car payments I was making toward achieving a new financial goal." One goal was to put $25,000 toward retirement in 2021.

"I didn't realize how much I could accomplish on my own once I had the correct tools in place. Being able to explain my financial situation to someone who is my age, has gone through similar financial struggles, and who provides nothing but support and encouragement was the boost I needed to make things happen."

If you think that she had to sacrifice enjoying her life to pay down the debt, think again! While Quinn was paying down her car, she also budgeted for a once-in-a-lifetime opportunity. "I set a goal to celebrate my thirty-sixth birthday on 2/22/22 by treating my close friends to a beautiful beach vacation in the Bahamas and the house has already been paid for!" I was so happy that she was able to live in the moment while investing in her future! Because she narrowed down her goals to what was most meaningful for her, she was able to finish them faster than if she'd juggled too many goals at once.

Let's Be Real about Why We Buy Expensive Cars

Man, oh man, do car companies know how to capitalize on the culture of instant gratification. Remember that client who told me that they were advised not to pay off their student loans so they could buy a nicer car? And remember who told them that? A car salesman!

Personally, the car I drive has little to no bearing on my personal identity, but I know for some, owning a luxury or expensive car is seen as a status symbol and a way to show others they are successful. I once was told by a client who lived in Silicon Valley that no one drives anything "less than a Tesla" there. Consciously or subconsciously, you may be prioritizing the image your car projects over its financial sense. For other people, cars can evoke strong emotional attachments, especially if they represent aspirations or dreams. For example, some people may be willing to overspend on a car they've always wanted, even if it means sacrificing financial stability.

Car manufacturers and dealerships are the masters of marketing tactics that promote expensive models and encourage you to upgrade to higher-end features you didn't even know existed. These marketing strategies create a desire for luxury, even when you know you may not be able to afford them comfortably. In particular, the now-easy access to financing options, such as long-term loans with low monthly payments, can make pricey cars feel more affordable on the surface.

However, I can't stress enough how important it is to understand the financial implications of car ownership, including the long-term costs of financing, maintenance, insurance, and depreciation. These payments may sound like deals at first, but they often come with high interest rates and long repayment terms, leading to higher overall costs in the long run.

Remember that a car is always depreciating—it will likely never be worth as much as you paid for it. Rather than hanging your identity on a piece of property that's losing its value daily, find other ways to boost your self-worth that are longer lasting. Getting into the habit of vesting fully in your future vehicles will help you drive with freedom, not just for looks.

RICH REFLECTIONS

Consider the concept of being "vested" in your vehicle. Do you currently own your car outright, or are you still making monthly payments? Find out how much you are paying in interest each month.

How does your car-ownership status affect your sense of financial security and freedom?

What factors are most important to you when choosing a car, such as reliability, fuel efficiency, or affordability? How do these factors align with your overall financial goals?

Reflect on any emotional or psychological factors that may influence your car-purchasing decisions. Do you feel pressure to own a certain type of car to maintain a certain image or status?

Explore three ways to minimize your car-related expenses, such as negotiating lower interest rates, shopping around for insurance quotes, or performing regular maintenance to prevent costly repairs. What steps can you take to optimize your car budget and maximize your financial resources?

THE HOME WITH HEART:
Spend for Security, Not Status

"Home is where the heart is," as the saying goes. But I wonder just how much heart is embedded in an American home nowadays, since home-ownership often feels more like a competition to keep up with neighbors or peers than it does to love where you live. For many people, a home purchase will be their largest asset purchase in their lifetime, so it's important to understand how your home fits into your overall net worth picture.

Bankrate's 2023 Financial Security survey reported that 74% of Americans consider homeownership to be of higher value than any other economic-stability measure, including a comfortable retirement, a successful career, having children, and holding a college degree. Pride is often cited as one of the main advantages of homeownership, since you have more freedom to express yourself in a house you own than you do in a rental.

When my father passed away, my beliefs toward homeownership were rocked to their core. My parents eventually owned their home outright, but my father didn't retire from his corporate career until his seventies, and he had little time for hobbies. I didn't learn he loved hiking and seeing shows until he wasn't as physically capable to enjoy those activities. I thought twice about whether I wanted to own my home and spend a bunch of time and money maintaining it, or prioritize having a smaller home and enjoying my freedom.

My question to you is this: Are you cultivating a gratitude attitude in how you perceive and treat your home? Regardless of whether you rent or own, being able to appreciate where you live now is a core component of a true financial-freedom plan. This is important because financial freedom is only authentic when you are loving where and how you live. Having a bigger, more beautiful home doesn't mean you are financially free. I have coached many clients who are convinced they need to buy a million-dollar home to be happy, without considering the true costs, whether it be more maintenance, longer commuting, or the constant social pressure to keep it perfect.

I sold my second paid-off home in 2021, and I've chosen to rent for the foreseeable future. I've learned to appreciate the benefits of having a smaller space with an on-site maintenance crew, instead of feeling "less than" my friends who own their homes. It's a misperception that a home-owner is more financially stable than a renter, as I have more in investments than most of my home-owning peers while also working way fewer hours.

Enjoy Renting for What It Offers

I recently watched a news story where a real estate expert exclaimed, "Rent is throwing money away." I've heard this same narrative from other financial experts, real estate agents, mortgage lenders, and even my own family and friends who are homeowners. This messaging contributed to my urgency in purchasing my first home in 2013, even though I was perfectly fine renting.

Since then, I've bought and sold three different homes. When I decided to rent again, it surprised all of our friends and my personal finance followers because I had paid off all three homes. I even asked my husband, "Is it crazy for us to rent again? Are we wasting money?"

But renting still offers a very basic benefit—a safe place to live, sleep, and store our possessions. The comparison is often made between renting a home and owning a home. But no one mentions the other comparison of renting a home versus not having one at all. For me, a home is not a part of my identity, but rather a basic need satisfied without having to purchase a property.

If you're a renter, don't feel ashamed for not owning a home! The financial sense of renting or buying depends a lot on where you prefer to live. According to an analysis by Realtor.com, in forty-five of the fifty largest US cities, renting costs less than buying a starter home. Despite rising costs, renting has become relatively more affordable than buying year over year.

Instead of comparing my smaller home to my friends' larger homes, I focus on the benefits that matter more to me. I live in Charlotte, North Carolina, where I have accessibility to restaurants, entertainment, and shopping within walking distance. I *could* buy another home on a thirty-year mortgage for cheaper than what I rent for right now, but it would require me to move twenty to thirty minutes away from my current address, and I wouldn't have walking access to those amenities that I really value. I sold my last home largely because location and convenience mattered to me more. That and AJ was sick and tired of mowing that dang lawn!

WHERE IS IT CHEAPER TO RENT THAN BUY?

The top five cities where it was cheaper to rent versus buy in 2023 were Austin, Texas; San Francisco, California; Seattle, Washington; Boston, Massachusetts; and Portland, Oregon. The job market profiles of these cities are vastly different from other larger metropolitan areas, since the local workforces are heavily powered by the tech industry. In contrast, the top five cities where it was cheaper to buy versus rent in 2023 were Memphis, Tennessee; Pittsburgh, Pennsylvania; Birmingham, Alabama; St. Louis, Missouri; and Baltimore, Maryland. In some of the more affordable real estate markets, a renter might find they will save cash each month by becoming a homeowner.

Consider How Your Home Helps You Reach Your Net Worth Goals

The largest gain I've had from the purchase of a real estate property was a little more than $250,000. But the investment of time I've put into my business has now given me the ability to generate $250,000 of revenue *annually*!

In 2019, my husband and I were proud outright owners of our home, having paid off our mortgage in our early thirties. I felt really confident in our decision going into 2020, when the COVID-19 pandemic shut down everything and our incomes became uncertain. I am still a huge proponent of paying off your mortgage early because of the peace it provided us.

In 2020, we bought a second home in the mountains, a small condo to escape from the city. By 2021 it was also paid off, and we officially passed $1 million in net worth for the first time, with the two homes as our biggest assets. What I didn't expect: Even though we had $1 million in assets, we had very little financial flexibility because our equity was tied up in the properties.

When we turned our eyes toward early retirement, we started looking for passive income. Our first inclination was to operate short-term rentals to create a new monthly stream of money. While this idea did bring in additional income, it didn't feel very passive—it was a lot of work and often inconvenient to manage the reservations and guests.

We could have taken out home equity loans from the homes to free up more cash, but we weren't comfortable with that risk during the pandemic uncertainty. Ultimately, we decided to sell both homes, and we applied the proceeds of those sales toward other financial vehicles, such as dividend exchange-traded funds (ETFs), treasury bills, and real estate investment trusts (REITs). Those investments now offer us similar monthly income that we can move much more easily than if we had to sell properties. I prefer the flexibility we have in moving our net worth, without affecting our living situation, as new investing opportunities arise.

Ask yourself this—are you using your home for security, or are you using it for social status? For us, renting has been a huge time and money saver. I no longer have to pay for gas to drive to a gym, a coffeehouse, or a pool because they are all an elevator ride away in my apartment building. Since I'm a business owner, I picked the particular building I live in so I could hold business meetings in the common area instead of meeting people at an office or coworking space that I'd have to pay for.

My Cash Flow Cushion now contains what I need for rent and utilities, and it requires thousands of dollars less than what I needed as a homeowner. I held on to savings in case my roof leaked again, or I decided to renovate my bathroom. The money I spent on appliances and furniture for a home now goes to international travel for speaking engagements and learning new technical skills.

Don't Make Being House Poor a Habit

Buying three homes helped me become a debt-free millionaire in my thirties, so I know it can be a good choice for some people. But I will say, it becomes hard to love where you live if your mortgage payments block you from affording much else in life. So how can you ensure you are best positioned financially if you do want to own a home? It first starts with the purchase.

I personally recommend that you set your purchasing budget to be half of what the bank approves. My husband and I stuck to this rule for the last three homes we bought because our goal is to become financially independent in our forties. When we bought our first home together, we were prequalified for at least a $200,000 purchase price on his salary and $400,000 using both our salaries.

Instead of going to the top of that price range for a much bigger home, we bought a home for half of what we were approved for. This allowed us to have a margin to pay off student loans, save for retirement, and pay off the home early. We also had peace of mind knowing that if one of us lost their income, we would still be able to make our house payments without too much strain.

One of the other rules I've stuck to is only buying a home with at least 20% down. Financial advisors, mortgage brokers, and real estate agents, however, will all assure you that you can put as little as 3.5% down on a thirty-year mortgage. According to the National Association of Realtors, the median US existing home sale price was $363,000 in February 2023. If you put down 20%, that means a down payment of $72,600.

I know putting down 20% is not easy, especially for home buyers juggling student loan debt, credit cards, family costs, and retirement savings. But if all you can afford is the minimum down payment, you're likely not in the best financial position to buy a home—yet. Committing to a goal of 20% down on a home required me to live well within my means and control spending, and it inspired me to grow my income over the years. It helped me build financial discipline and taught me how to choose long-term stability over short-term comfort.

When you pay a low amount for a down payment on a home or when you finance it over thirty years, the bulk of your monthly payments will be to cover interest and private mortgage insurance, anyway.

THE THIRTY-YEAR MORTGAGE IS AN INTEREST TRAP

I opted to finance my past three homes on ten- or fifteen-year mortgages rather than thirty-year options. The lower interest rates and the shorter repayment periods have saved me hundreds of thousands of dollars in interest and allowed me to pay off the homes even faster than the mortgage durations. Here's an example. Let's take that $363,000 median home price. If you were to buy that home today with a 20% down payment, you'd have to finance $290,400. On a thirty-year mortgage with an 8% interest rate, the monthly payment would be $2,131, but the total interest paid would be $476,706 over the thirty years.

Now take that same down payment on a fifteen-year mortgage. With the same interest rate, the total interest paid would be $209,138 with a monthly payment of $2,775. That difference of $644 per month is certainly a challenge, but it would save $267,568 and fifteen years of payments. That could be enough money to buy another home!

Make It a Habit to Love Where You Live

Homeownership has often been the symbol of the American dream. But you can end up feeling house poor, even with a beautiful home, if you can't afford to do much else. As the children of immigrants, and as millennials, my husband and I felt the constant pressure from our families and friends to "settle down." Our parents were eager to show their friends that they had raised responsible adults, and we wanted to show our friends how "successful" we were.

My husband bought his first home in 2009 and unexpectedly moved two years later, which resulted in him having to pay $10,000 to sell the home. If you're financing your purchase with a mortgage and not reasonably certain you'll stay for the next five years, you risk losing money if you need to sell your home or if its value decreases because you haven't built much equity yet.

We ended up buying a 2,200-square-foot, four-bedroom home and lived there for eight years. We were constantly fixing it up, mowing the lawn we barely used, and filling the rooms up with furniture and decor. As I mentioned, it turns out we didn't actually enjoy homeownership, and to everyone's surprise, we sold our third and last paid-off home in 2022 and went back to renting. For us, that meant living on our own terms rather than our loan terms, and we love where we live even if we don't own it.

The lesson here isn't to only rent or to only buy—it's to express daily gratitude for the home you live in, regardless of how it's paid for. I encourage you to incorporate gratitude for your home while you work on your net worth goals and curate your accounts, even if you plan on living somewhere else in the future.

RICH REFLECTIONS

Are you satisfied with your housing situation, or do you feel pressure to meet societal expectations?

What aspects of your living space are you most grateful for, and how can you cultivate a deeper sense of appreciation for your current home?

Explore your motivations for pursuing homeownership. Are you seeking security, social status, or a combination of both? How do these motivations influence your financial decisions?

Consider the concept of "house poor" and how it relates to your personal finances. Are you prioritizing homeownership at the expense of other financial goals or experiences?

Reflect on any past experiences or decisions related to housing that have shaped your current perspective. What lessons have you learned, and how can you apply them to make more informed housing choices in the future?

THE REAL LUXURY BAGS:
Make Retirement Investing a Habit

My luxury bags aren't called Louis, Chanel, or Prada. They're called 401(k), traditional IRA, and Roth IRA. If you live in the United States and you want to retire at all, let alone early, you need to level up your investing habits, sis! The good news is that more women are investing than ever before. In fact, according to a 2021 study by Charles Schwab, 15% of all investors started in 2020. So, the message is getting out that investing is important.

The challenge is that many people begin investing based on generic advice, without fully understanding what they're investing into and how they can be most efficient; this is a trend I've seen among many of my CRUSH Bootcamp members. Investing is a long-term habit that requires patience and persistence, and it will be easier to maintain this habit if you get clear on how to invest without overcomplicating it.

Pay Off Your Debt Before Investing More

This is the most common question I get: Should I pay off debt or invest? I know I sound like a broken record, but I have and always will stand by paying off debt first. Remember, debt is meant to be a short-term solution. It is not, in my opinion, meant to be a long-term lifestyle. Financial advisors have tricked us into thinking we're foolish if we choose to pay off low-interest debt, but it's essential to remember that financial institutions want us to be their passive income. They get passive income from you paying interest to them in the form of debt. And they get passive income from you by convincing you to invest with them and taking a piece of your hard-earned money for essentially no work on their part.

If you treat debt as a short-term solution, then once you're done, you're done. And then you have the option to invest all that money that used to be the bank's passive income. Interestingly enough, the fear of missing out on investing motivated me to pay off my debt even faster so that I could get to investing as soon as possible. The process came with many trade-offs, including downsizing from two cars to one, forgoing some vacations, living off of one income instead of two, and carefully budgeting our daily expenses.

There were definitely swaps in our discretionary expenses that many of our friends thought we were overly frugal about. But my husband and I surprised ourselves by paying off that $72,000 debt in one year instead of two, and the experience encouraged me to exhaust all other options before ever taking on debt again.

We also feel so much relief knowing we have fewer debt accounts to manage. Once I built the courage to leave my day job, I opened up my own 401(k) through my business to also max out, match myself, and contribute more to profit sharing. We now have contributed at least $50,000 on an annual basis since becoming debt-free—a huge increase from the $6,000 per year we would have contributed had we stayed in debt.

Base Investing Decisions on Actual Dollars, Not Just Interest Rates

A common trap people fall into is choosing to invest when they have debt because of what they think is simple math. They're often told by financial advisors that their interest rates are low, but the returns on investments like stocks are higher.

It *seems* like simple math to compare interest rates and thus invest versus paying off debt. But when you actually plug in dollar amounts, you might realize you're losing more money than you think. Some of my millennial peers have carried their student loans into middle age and might even do so into retirement. Borrowers ages thirty-five to forty-nine make up the highest number of people owing more than $100,000. In 2016, two months after completing graduate school, I resolved that I would pay off my $72,000 of student loans in two years instead of ten.

Using a student loan interest calculator, I learned my loans (with an average interest rate of 4%) were accruing $7.92 daily. I was shocked because I thought the interest accrued monthly, as with my savings account. I also realized that as a beginner investor with only a few hundred dollars to spare each month, it was highly unlikely I would find an investment option that would earn me the same interest or appreciation ($7.92 a day) that I was paying in student loan interest.

A low interest rate on a high dollar amount of debt will add up to more money than you think. You can verify this by looking at your various debt statements and finding the dollar amounts you are actually paying, not just the interest rates, and then ask yourself if you could make those same dollar amounts on investments. Paying down your debt is a guaranteed return—you will see your total debt drop and your net worth rise. You also save the amount you would have paid in interest when you pay extra toward your debt. On the other hand, any investment is a risk—the return isn't guaranteed.

Save Thousands in Taxes on Your Investments

Would you like to pay more in taxes than you need to? Of course, the answer is heck no, but so many people are doing just that based on what kinds of accounts they're putting their investments in. I know this because in looking at hundreds of people's finances, I see them putting money into investment accounts that cost them more in taxes than they need to pay.

The simplest strategy you can have is to use the accounts that cost you way less in taxes than others do. These are called tax-advantaged accounts, and they are usually in the form of retirement accounts in the United States, such as a 401(k), a 403(b), or an individual retirement account (IRA). In fact, I will even say that you don't need any other investment accounts until you have absolutely exhausted the limits of these accounts.

TRADITIONAL RETIREMENT ACCOUNTS OFFER TAX SAVINGS NOW

A traditional retirement account provides tax savings today by lowering the amount of income you are being taxed on in a given calendar year. This is also known as a tax deduction. Other tax deductions you might be familiar with are mortgage interest, contributing to charity, and health insurance payments.

There are two types of retirement accounts that you need to know about. They are "traditional" and "Roth" and there is one key difference between the two: when you get the tax benefit. Traditional accounts help you save on taxes today, whereas Roth accounts have tax benefits in retirement. The easy way to remember is their first letters: "T" = traditional = today, and "R" = Roth = retirement. Unlike a general investment account (also called a brokerage account), which you might encounter on apps such as Robinhood or Acorns, both traditional and Roth contributions save you money on taxes.

So, if your annual income is $70,000 and you contribute $10,000 to a traditional retirement account this year, your taxable income for this year is considered to be $60,000. The $10,000 you put in your retirement investments is not taxed. When you take funds out during retirement, you will owe income taxes on the withdrawal based on your income and tax bracket at that time. This includes all of the earnings your investments grew over the years.

CONSIDER HOW MUCH YOU CAN AFFORD NOW VERSUS LATER

Whether you contribute to a traditional or Roth retirement account also depends on how much money you need for other current expenses, particularly if you are carrying high-interest credit card debt, saving to buy a home, or paying off student loans.

If you are deciding whether to contribute the same amount to your retirement via traditional or Roth options, your take-home pay will be higher if you choose traditional contributions. Having more disposable cash now may be more important for you depending on your current budget and long-term financial plans. This is why stacking the budgeting habits with your investing habits is absolutely critical. Budgeting will help you find extra dollars to contribute to your retirement investing while making sure you don't find yourself short on paying your bills in the present. (Keep in mind that both traditional and Roth accounts have specific withdrawal rules that include potential tax implications and penalties if you need to access that money before retirement age.)

A Roth retirement account saves you taxes in retirement and on your investment growth. Roth retirement contributions require you to pay the taxes now at your current tax bracket. Using the same numbers as before, if your income for the year is $70,000, and you contribute $10,000, you will still pay taxes on your total $70,000 salary now, assuming no other deductions. However, the magic of a Roth account is that when you withdraw funds in retirement, you won't owe taxes on any of the money. More importantly (and what most people misunderstand), you also won't pay taxes on the earnings you've made since your original contributions. If you can accommodate contributing more toward a Roth account, you can save the headache of taxes further down the road.

To clarify, if the $10,000 you contributed in a traditional retirement account grows to $30,000 when you retire, you will pay taxes on the entire $30,000 as you withdraw, including the $20,000 of growth. But if you contribute it to a Roth account, you will not pay taxes on the $20,000 of growth. This means that income earned on the account, from interest, dividends, or capital gains, is tax-free, according to the US Securities and Exchange Commission.

If It's Not a True Emergency, Keep Your Luxury Bags Full

A record number of Americans used their 401(k) plans in 2022 and 2023 for hardship withdrawals. This type of early withdrawal can help if you face emergencies like medical crises or eviction. However, since the COVID-19 pandemic, I have seen people withdrawing for nonemergency expenses to start businesses, buy cars, or purchase discretionary items.

Unfortunately, in our twenties, my husband and I thought of our retirement accounts as a black hole for our money and decided to start using them. I regret how we took tens of thousands of dollars out of retirement savings to buy an investment property, because back then we weren't financially or emotionally mature enough to make good investment choices. Even with a tax bill and a 10% early-withdrawal penalty, we cared more about short-term gratification than long-term benefits and decided to withdraw the money. We simply followed general trends and generic advice, even when those didn't necessarily make sense for us.

Carla Paid Off Debt and Saved Enough to Retire and Fulfill Her Purpose

The year 2023 proved to be full of surprises for Carla, one of my early CRUSH Bootcamp members who I still stay closely connected with. Her son's birth mom passed away, causing a ripple effect on her son and family. With this huge challenge, Carla was unable to work. She ended up with credit card debt because shopping was her unhealthy coping mechanism, as she put it.

Then she gave herself some grace and reconnected with her support system—me and the CRUSH Bootcamp. Carla acknowledged—without judgment—that she had taken some steps backward...because life happens. With a little bit of coaching and a great deal of focus, the stars aligned and allowed Carla to not only pay off her debt but leave her corporate role after seventeen years in financial services. Carla had also been running a business on the side, something she was really passionate about—supporting families impacted by mental health conditions, community and gun violence, and trauma. She offers them help as someone with training, but more importantly—lived experience. But she was stressed out about her family and trying to balance her corporate job with her purpose-based work.

She worked her financial plan and made sure that she had over $1 million invested, to use for retirement, insurance for her family, and a cushion by which she could launch her business as a full-time entrepreneur. She saw a need, a gap, in support for her community. And she is fulfilling that need.

Once again free of credit card debt, Carla was able to focus on managing her mortgage and student loans. "Working with Bernadette enabled me to start thinking more about early retirement to really digging into my heart work, which involves speaking engagements, workshops, moderating discussions about being trauma informed and trauma resiliency," Carla said. "I am doing my part to stomp out the stigma of mental health [conditions]." When you see Carla smiling, you know that it's because she really loves what she does and sees her impact in the communities she serves—while successfully caring for her family at the same time!

Since then, we've committed to learning and understanding the tenets of financial independence and calculating how much we need to retire at all, let alone early. Now that I know and understand how retirement plans work, I don't recommend doing that for a discretionary purchase that you could save up for instead.

We each regularly contribute the maximum allowed by the IRS to our retirement accounts. And if we ever have cash flow issues, rather than withdraw, we plan to pause our contributions instead. Now we look at the purpose of tax-advantaged accounts as saving up for our future selves and helping us save on taxes that we otherwise would have to pay in regular brokerage accounts.

If you're craving more advice on how and what to invest in, that's a great sign! I've shared some of my favorite resources on this topic in the back of this book. The bottom line is this: By reframing your retirement accounts as your real luxury bags, rather than the boring accounts most of us ignore, you can become a great investor without overcomplicating your strategy. Intentionally and consistently sending money into a retirement account versus a regular brokerage account will save you thousands upon thousands of dollars that you can pay to yourself instead of the government. It's the best place to start investing and keep a long-term investing habit.

RICH REFLECTIONS

Reflect on past financial decisions, particularly those related to investing. What lessons have you learned from these experiences, and how can they inform your future investment strategy?

Imagine you had zero debt. How would that impact your ability to invest more into your future self?

How does reframing your perspective on investing and retirement accounts as your "real luxury bags" empower you to take control of your financial future with confidence and clarity?

How can you cultivate patience to stay focused on your long-term investing habit, even in the face of short-term temptations?

What additional knowledge or expertise do you need to make informed investment decisions? What questions do you have? Write them down and commit to finding those answers in the next thirty days.

THE NEGOTIATION NORM:
Stop Settling for Less Pay

Most people are aware of the persisting gender wage gap. According to the Pew Research Center, the gender gap in pay in the US has barely moved over the past twenty years. In 2022, women earned an average of 82% of what men earned, while women earned 80% as much as men in 2002. I've mentioned this stat earlier, and I'll repeat it again to remind us that we're not progressing as fast as we need for women.

The less publicized disparity that we need to fight to close is the gender *wealth* gap. The most prominent reports show that for every dollar a white man owns, women overall own just 32 cents. For every $1 of wealth owned by a single white man, single Black women and single Latinas own 9 cents. The wealth gap is not just about salary—it includes how much we own in total, including the value of assets such as cash, investments, and real estate, minus debts.

Without actively working to increase our pay, women will never close the wealth gap. (In particular, women of color too often set lower pay requirements than white men.) I saw this firsthand when I worked for several financial services firms and tech startups, where I spent ten years in human resources and recruiting roles. And I can count on one hand the number of times a woman negotiated pay with me.

Now, as a money coach, I field questions like this from fellow women: "I have been working at this company for several years now. And I know for a fact that I am underpaid for my job. I know this because I do pay ranges for other people's jobs, and I am well below the median. I would like to have a discussion with my manager to discuss a pay raise and I don't know how to start."

Negotiating pay is easier said than done, especially if you're a woman battling impostor syndrome. Regardless of your race or gender, though, I want to share my top secrets as a former recruiter. These tips will help you practice with confidence. Aim to negotiate your pay every year, even if you don't think you'll get it. The cost of not negotiating is too damn high, individually and collectively, for women. Making negotiation your norm rather than the exception will leapfrog your net worth numbers closer to the freedom you deserve.

Use a Very Specific Number When Asked for Your Ideal Salary

I read a 2013 study from Columbia Business School that showed that if you use, for example, $50,750 as a number that you're going into a negotiation with, instead of $50,000, guess what? It makes you present yourself as assertive, smarter, and much more informed. As a recruiter, when an employee or prospective candidate used a more specific and precise number in their initial negotiation request, I was more likely to get the final offer closer to what the person requested. It made me believe the candidate was coming from a place of information, research, and competence and not just pulling a number out of the blue.

How do you pick that specific number? It can be based on research from reputable online sources that give pay ranges for the job that you are in. But it can also simply be based on your own needs. For example, if you are buying a new home and you know that your mortgage payment is going to increase by $100, then increase the job pay that you're looking for by that amount. Or it could be my favorite number: How much debt do you want to pay off this year? Your employer or business-deal partner doesn't need to know that's the reason. The simplicity of being specific will rarely get pushback. When you ask for a specific number, they assume you've done your homework.

DON'T GET TRAPPED IN THE FALLACY OF GETTING PAID FOR A FORTY-HOUR WORK WEEK

If your negotiations for higher pay fail, work less. Sounds crazy, but by law, if you are a salaried employee, your employer cannot dictate how many hours you work. If they do dictate hours, the employer is legally obligated to pay you overtime. If you're getting pay that's lower than you want, consider how you can do that job in fewer hours. And no, you don't need your company's permission or to broadcast that you are working less.

Get Loud on LinkedIn

I've interviewed hundreds of candidates over the years and have found that women have a really hard time bragging about their skills and what they've accomplished. If you are going for a pay negotiation, you must be willing to document and speak to what you've already accomplished, not just what you think you can bring in the future. LinkedIn is the perfect place to document your accomplishments because it is public, whereas your résumé and performance reviews are private.

As an Asian American and an introvert, it's a struggle for me to advocate for myself because it feels like bragging. So, I've made it a habit to update my LinkedIn profile quarterly in the following ways:

- Changing the headline and summary section based on my most recent accomplishments
- Asking for recommendations from happy clients and partners
- Sharing content that I think best showcases my expertise

Updating your LinkedIn page also sends a clear signal to your current or potential employer that you are not afraid to share with prospective employers who are looking for you. The days of unquestioned loyalty as an employee are dead. It's okay to let your employer or business partners know it's a two-way street.

One of the best features of LinkedIn is the option to post recommendations. It shows that a real person took the time to write a recommendation for you that would be publicly shared, and it feels more credible. I have more than fifteen recommendations on my LinkedIn profile that have gotten me business opportunities that I otherwise wouldn't have acquired. It's a strategic way of saying you're awesome...without actually having to say it yourself.

Thanks to this consistent habit, I've had more opportunities come my way versus having to hunt them down, because the people in my network are getting a slow, consistent drip of what I do best and they have the proof to back it up, not just a once-off conversation. Rather than waiting until the point at which you need to negotiate to show off your best work, doing it year-round will make it feel less awkward when the moment comes. Or better yet, you may not have to say as much, because your network will already know.

Use Your Résumé As a Straightforward Script

If you spend a lot of time trying to sound smart on your résumé, hiring managers and recruiters will probably know you are trying as well. Most résumés I've read are filled with unnecessary fluff that could be more succinctly summarized with action verbs and accomplishments. They also almost always include words that would sound awkward or stiff if you actually read your résumé out loud. For example, it's unlikely you would say, "I work independently" or "I am an enthusiastic team player with excellent written communication skills."

If your résumé is streamlined and conversational, it can then provide key talking points to keep right in front of you during a negotiation. They'll remind your employer why you deserve more pay. In lieu of fluff phrases, incorporate concise reasons why paying you more in salary would actually mean more money for the company, such as:

- How your contributions increased revenue
- How you improved processes to cut back on expenses
- How you can be more efficient and get things done faster than your peers

Expectations from hiring managers are higher than ever, but their attention spans are also shorter than ever. Instead of writing your résumé to just be read by the hiring team, read it out loud and write it as if you were talking naturally during an interview. And please, no two-page résumés. Keep yours to one page, no matter how long you've worked. Remember that by keeping an updated résumé handy at all times, you are reducing the risk of depleting your Keep Calm Fund in the event you need to find a new job!

A Personal Success Story: Don't Rule Out Negotiating Employee Offers Into Consulting Work

A company that courted me for years wanted me to be an employee. They offered me $85,000 simply because the person who had just left the job made that much at forty hours a week. I considered the time and energy that it would require for me to deliver what she did, and I knew I didn't need forty hours to do the job well.

I said, "I would still love to work with you, but as a consultant. I'm happy to take the $85,000, but I'll make my own hours and still run my own business." The CEO said, "I don't know how that's going to work. How can you run your business and also work for us?"

I said, "Would you be asking me this if, instead of running a business, we were talking about raising kids? Let's try it out for six months. And if you don't like what I'm doing, we can both end the contract six months from now."

I got so efficient at this role that I was working maybe ten hours a week for the same amount of pay that the employer gave someone else to work forty hours a week. At the end of the six months, they still wanted to pay me the same rate and continue the opportunity.

The Most Effective Strategy: Set Your Finances Up for the Freedom to Walk Away

This is your biggest tool in any negotiation. You need to be willing and able to walk away. When considering your numbers, you need a walk-away point—an offer that you have to turn down. This can be based on your financial need, your market value, or simply what you need to feel good about the pay that you're bringing home.

Of course, you know by now that I strongly advocate getting your personal finances in order, particularly paying down all consumer debt, so you can have three months' worth of expenses saved in your Keep Calm Fund. Being debt-free now for years, I have the confidence to walk away from any job in which the offer doesn't match my needs or expectations. Having your Keep Calm Fund, your Cash Flow Cushion, and your net worth organized and in order gives you the runway to wait for the right opportunity to come along, and to not have to accept anything less than what you and your talents are worth.

RICH REFLECTIONS

Explore your past experiences with negotiation. Have you negotiated your pay in the past? If so, how did it go? What lessons did you learn from those experiences?

Consider the potential risks of not negotiating your pay. How might staying silent impact your financial future, career progression, and overall satisfaction in your job?

Imagine your ideal outcome from a successful negotiation. What changes would a higher pay bring to your life and career? How would it align with your goals and aspirations?

Identify sources of support and encouragement in your network. Who can provide guidance, advice, or mentorship as you navigate the negotiation process?

What strategies can you employ to overcome anxiety and assert yourself effectively? How can you prepare and practice for a successful negotiation?

6

Spend Intentionally

I have a confession: I'm a reformed shopaholic. As in, I actually thought that retail therapy was a fair replacement for actual therapy. While I was working at my soul-sucking banking job at a company I'll call Moldcan Racks, I would take my paychecks and spend them along the famous Fifth Avenue in New York City. But because I am a deal shopper, I honestly thought that buying clothes at 50% off meant I was saving money.

I counted once, and I had seventy-two dresses in my closet that I'd worn once, maybe twice at best. Maybe you also had that season in your life when you were invited to two dozen weddings and couldn't dare to wear the same dress twice. So, instead, you spent all your money on clothes, money that could have been your retirement fund. Or maybe you were smart like my longtime friend, who borrowed said dresses from silly friends like me and just paid for dry cleaning. She became a millionaire faster by investing that money instead of spending it on dresses. (Yes, that really did happen. I'm still jealous of that friend for being so much freaking smarter than I was.)

The "S" in CRUSH stands for "spend intentionally" and refers to making deliberate and thoughtful choices about how you allocate your financial resources. It challenges you to align your spending habits with your personal values, priorities, and long-term goals. Spending intentionally requires you to:

- Prioritize value over price, considering factors such as quality, durability, and long-term benefits when making purchasing decisions

- Resist the urge to make unplanned or unnecessary purchases (even if it's a great deal), considering whether that deal aligns with what you said you were going to do
- Carefully consider whether the spending is beneficial to your overall well-being instead of increasing spending as your income rises
- Recognize who you are as a unique individual instead of falling prey to societal expectations, lifestyle inflation, and really clever marketing

Overall, spending intentionally involves a mindful approach to managing money, aiming to maximize satisfaction and fulfillment while minimizing waste and unnecessary expenses.

But if you're expecting these next five habits to shame you for making dumb spending choices in the past, breathe easy. I'm in no position to point fingers without being a total hypocrite!

However, if you're looking for practical strategies on how to still live in a modern world and face the reality that yes, consumption culture is not going away any time soon, I've got great news for you. This is exactly the chapter to help you learn to love spending in a healthy way without having to shun all your prized possessions.

THE $1 RULE:
The Secret to Guilt-Free Shopping

When I was drowning in debt and burned out at my day job, I knew I needed a plan—except I didn't want to follow the traditional scrimp-and-save method.

Many experts offer the advice to cut out unnecessary expenses, adhere to a super-strict budget, and work yourself to the bone until you pay off your debt. But constantly tracking every penny and slapping myself on the wrist didn't make me want to spend less—it just made me feel worse about when I did spend money, even when it was on something that brought me joy.

Instead, my husband and I did the opposite: We became adamant about spending on the things we really loved and instead cut back on the things that were nice to have, impulse buys, just convenient in the moment, or simply unimportant.

We did this in part by implementing the $1 Rule: only buying things that cost $1 or less per use. With the help of this one habit, I've managed to pay off debt and keep on track with ambitious financial goals to save enough for retirement thirty years ahead of schedule—without going back to my old spending habits.

How to Apply the $1 Rule

The $1 Rule is simple. It's a very specific version of a term you might know already: "cost per use." To calculate cost per use, you take the price of an item and divide the cost by the number of times you use it. If a gadget costs $200 and you use it four times, the cost per use is $50.

When I'm on one of my shopping sprees, I simplify even more so that I can make decisions more quickly. If an item comes out to $1 or less per use, I give myself the green light to buy it. No analysis paralysis or asking for opinions on whether to buy it. I just buy it and move on with my life.

This rule works especially well when applied to my weak spots where I tend to binge: clothing, accessories, and home goods. You may be surprised to hear this, but I'm the money coach who loves all things fashion, and I won't discourage you from clothes shopping, as long as you use this rule to keep it in check! Growing up in New York City, sneakers became my love language. I recently purchased a pair of pink-and-black Nike Dunks for $50 on sale. Before buying them, I calculated that I would probably wear them once a week for a year, or at least fifty-two times. My guess was right: In the last three months, I've already worn them more than twice a week, coming out to less than $1 per wear faster than my anticipated year to make them "worth it."

During the same shopping trip, I found a beautiful fluffy skirt that was also on clearance, marked down from $150 to $35. While I was lured in by the big discount and brand name, I stopped to do the math. I considered the number of special occasions that I could wear this pink puffy skirt to, and I couldn't see myself wearing it thirty-five times—and therefore, it wasn't worth the money. I walked away and left it on the rack.

The $1 Rule gives you permission to still buy things you use frequently, while preventing impulse purchases just because they seem like a good deal. It also encourages spending more on high-quality, classic, and sustainable items that will last. I've moved almost entirely away from fast fashion, because even a $5 shirt that I might wear only once breaks the $1 Rule.

How to Use the $1 Rule on Major Items

Traditional debt-free advice discourages buying anything, especially big-ticket items. Instead, I implement the $1 Rule when debating major expenses, like furniture or technology. Expensive items look different when you consider them from a "per use" perspective.

When we bought our last home, it became clear that my old HGTV-obsessed self was making a comeback. It's easy to get so swept up in the excitement of decorating a new home that you buy more than you really need.

But what is actually *worth* the money?

With both my husband and me working from home permanently, we decided we were willing to pay a little more for quality desks and office chairs, because that's where we spend most of our time. We also learned from previous moves that cheaper desks tend to fall apart easily.

Instead of going to Target or getting desks from Craigslist like we'd done before, we went to a higher-quality furniture outlet. We found a classic desk that retailed for $699, marked down 40% to $419. That was much more than I'd ever spent on a desk, but using the $1 Rule, I realized I would sit in front of it five days a week for fifty weeks a year, which is 250 uses per year. The purchase would pass the $1 Rule in less than two years.

WHAT IF SOMETHING DOESN'T PASS THE $1 RULE?

Of course, I still have the occasional splurge or impulse purchase. It's typically not on material things, but activities I enjoy with my family and friends in my spare time. For example, while I was focused on paying off my student loans and mortgage, the Broadway show *Hamilton* came to our city. The former New Yorker and musical theater geek in me was conflicted with the voices of prominent debt experts saying that buying these very expensive tickets would be stupid. And while I almost always stick with the $1 Rule, I make a few very personal exceptions.

I did buy the *Hamilton* tickets and had no regrets. What many debt experts wouldn't relate to is that, for me, Broadway was the only place I saw another Filipino American represented, thanks to the famous Broadway actress Lea Salonga. You can't put a price on representation when you were deprived of it your whole childhood. I was easily willing to swap expenses like food and social gatherings to stay within my budget that month so I could pay for the tickets in full, without a credit card.

Yes, the tickets broke the $1 Rule, since I only saw the show once, but the occasional "unnecessary" item isn't going to completely derail a financial plan. I've since seen the show two more times, and the last time I saw it, the actor who played the lead role was Filipino! The pride I felt was worth every penny!

I'm not a big fan of luxury brands nowadays, as I have found that the prices have skyrocketed while the quality has deteriorated significantly over the past decade. I've seen $10,000 items wear down after just a few uses. However, I do own a handful of mid-range and higher-priced handbags that met the $1 Rule because my intention was to keep them for decades, not just a season.

The $1 Rule is a great motivator for keeping your wardrobe timeless, because those $1 uses can stretch over years to come as long as the pieces stay in great condition. I feel much more confident in my purchases than I did in the days when I used to scrimp and save every penny.

This area is where I think most people's idea of living debt-free is wrong. Who can give up all the fun spending and have nothing to look forward to? I sacrifice on other things and narrow down the few items that I absolutely love—musical theater, K-pop concerts, and travel—and spend unapologetically on them, even if other people don't agree with my choices. These few exceptions kept me focused on the long and often monotonous journey of paying off debt, while removing the guilt of spending on things that were meaningful to me.

How the $1 Rule Can Help You Decrease Debt

The original intent of my $1 Rule was to curb spending on frivolous and unnecessary purchases and help me focus on my debt. It's worked so well that my husband and I have been able to stop using a credit card during our debt-free journey. I used to think, *How many credit card points will I earn on this purchase?* But now I ask, *Does this purchase fit the $1 Rule?*

Something unexpected happened too: The $1 Rule removed the shame that other personal finance advice often made me feel for spending on something, even if I really needed it. Last year, my four-year-old phone started to fail. The thought of unexpectedly having to spend hundreds of dollars on a new phone nearly threw me into a panic attack. It felt like a huge setback in my quest to save money.

I was complaining about how my phone wouldn't even turn on anymore, and a member of my CRUSH Bootcamp said, "Stop it! If you need it, you need it. Don't make it a thing!" She reminded me that the phone, while expensive, clearly got the green light under my $1 Rule. (Even a money coach like me has to be reminded that spending on something you'll use all the time is okay, even if it costs a pretty penny!)

I've seen this scarcity mentality in myself and other people in the debt-free community. We get so focused on how much things cost that we become afraid to spend anything at all.

The $1 Rule has not only kept me from spending on things I don't need but removed guilt and debate when spending on things I do need.

RICH REFLECTIONS

Describe a situation where you felt guilty or anxious about a necessary purchase before implementing the $1 Rule. How can the rule help alleviate those feelings?

Explore the concept of scarcity mentality (in other words, the mindset characterized by a belief in limited resources, leading to feelings of competition or fear of loss) and its impact on your financial habits. How can the $1 Rule help you overcome this mindset?

Consider how the $1 Rule can shift your focus from short-term gratification to long-term financial goals. How will this change in perspective affect your overall financial health?

What in your home does not fit the $1 Rule? What will you do differently next time you shop?

What have you bought that fits the $1 Rule? Write how that was a great purchase you don't regret!

THE DECLUTTER-THE-DATE CHALLENGE:
Clear Space for New Money

Get ready for one of my favorite practical money habits, which the CRUSH Bootcamp showed me can also be fun and rewarding: getting rid of extra possessions in order to curb your future spending and focus on saving time, energy, and money.

Was anyone else obsessed with Marie Kondo like me? I bought into the whole joy of tidying up after reading her book and watching her television series. My jeans were folded into neat little thirds, and I quickly tossed out anything that didn't bring me joy. I credit Marie Kondo for finally getting me to part ways with a thirty-pound box of old photo albums from high school that I carted around the country with me on my various moves. When I finally opened that one sentimental box and went through the photos, I realized I didn't even remember or like most of the people pictured in them and reduced that box down to one folder of photos. I'm sure you've heard of plenty of decluttering techniques and why you should scale back what you own...but have you thought about just how much your collection of stuff is affecting your ability to make better money choices? Chances are, if you're reading this book and trying to get good with money, you know there are material items you've spent money on that are now also cluttering up your mind and your space. Don't worry, I'm not shaming you—and you're definitely not alone. According to research commissioned by Ladder and conducted by OnePoll, the average adult in the US spends $1,497 a month on nonessential items. That's roughly $18,000 a year on things we can all do without!

How to Start the Challenge

The Declutter-the-Date Challenge is essentially asking you to clear out a certain number of items each day for a month, based on the calendar date. You're aiming to declutter and make space for a lighter, more intentional life and to face the reality of what you've spent your hard-earned money on that no longer brings you joy.

The challenge is easy to understand but gets tougher to stick to as the month goes on. On day one, say March 1, declutter one thing. On March 2, declutter two things. On March 3, toss three things. You get the idea. Even if you read about this challenge in the middle of the month, you can still start then and try to catch up by getting rid of the number of things you need to clear out from the days you missed. Simple, right?

EAT THE FROG

There's a phrase I love that says to "eat the frog"—basically, just swallow your pride and do the hard thing. On the first day of my own Declutter-the-Date Challenge, I found a fairly expensive purple furry top and realized there was nothing I owned that I could wear with it that looked good. Sometimes, you just have to eat the frog and let that thing you've been holding on to leave your home so you can make space for all the fun things your new money habits will afford you!

For example, if you're the pantry-stocking type, the month in which you are doing the challenge is the perfect time to use those ingredients and clear out your pantry. I always meet new members who spend a ton on eating out when they have a fully stocked pantry and refrigerator at home, and the Declutter-the-Date Challenge is a perfect habit to pair with the Lean Kitchen.

Decluttering in Small Chunks Adds Up to Big Change

Imagine this: My members who stuck to the challenge for all twenty-nine days in February 2024 and decluttered physical items daily were able to clear 435 items! That's the sum of all the numbers 1 through 29. Picture how much lighter and freer you'd feel without 435 unnecessary items in your life.

The beauty of the Declutter-the-Date Challenge, especially while you're building smart money habits, is that it builds up via a snowball effect. It's similar to tackling debt using the snowball method. The debt snowball method is a debt-reduction strategy where you focus on paying off your smallest debts first while making minimum payments on larger debts, then once the smallest debt is paid off, you roll the amount you were paying on it into the next smallest debt, creating a snowball effect until all debts are paid off. The dopamine rush I got from tackling my debt snowball is the same satisfaction I got with Declutter-the-Date. You start off small, you build up your snowball over the course of the month, and without even realizing it, you've cleared out some space!

DON'T OWN THAT MUCH?

Now, for those of you with minimal clutter, I get it. You might not have tons of extra stuff to declutter creatively. No worries—here's an alternative: Pay off that amount in debt. Instead of decluttering twenty-five items on March 25, pay $25 toward your debt instead. Think of each of those dollars in your debt accounts as individual items that also need to be cleared from your money plan and your life. If you're tackling debt instead, by doing it daily, you'd pay off $496 in that month of March. That's real progress!

When you start small, it seems manageable at first. The first couple of days aren't too challenging, right? But around day thirteen or fourteen, that's when reality kicks in. Finding fourteen things to declutter suddenly feels like a mission. And remember, donating is not the only way to clear things out of your home. You can repurpose, use up, and sell stuff too.

If you really want to get crazy with this habit, try it each month for a full year. Guess how many items that would be or how many dollars in debt you would pay off:

MONTH	DAYS	ITEMS
January	31	496
February	28	406
March	31	496
April	30	465
May	31	496
June	30	465
July	31	496

MONTH	DAYS	ITEMS
August	31	496
September	30	465
October	31	496
November	30	465
December	31	496
TOTAL		**5,738**

And here's why we're doing this in a book about money. There's a certain revelation we all experience when we gather the stuff we spent money on and realize it's about to leave our lives. That moment of, *Wow, I spent so much on this.* It's a powerful reminder to be mindful about your spending and not buy more junk that will only get decluttered later. Even if you only do it every now and then, this game is a way to reset the intentions you have for the other money habits you are building along the way. Hack this habit by finding a few friends who will do it with you and share your progress on social media with #DeclutterTheDate, and consider sharing a winner prize or a celebratory meal when you finish!

RICH REFLECTIONS

Reflect on a recent purchase that no longer brings you joy. Why did you buy it, and how do you feel about it now?

Is there an item you've been holding on to that you know you need to part ways with?

Explore the connection between clutter and your financial habits. How does clutter impact your ability to make better money choices?

How can you repurpose or creatively use items you no longer need instead of simply discarding them?

Imagine the end result of completing the challenge. How would your mindset and living space be transformed, and how would this impact your confidence in making money decisions?

THE LEAN KITCHEN:
Nourish Your Financial Health

In your quest for financial freedom, every aspect of your life is an opportunity to practice spending intentionally. Surprisingly, one area often overlooked in this pursuit is the kitchen. I'm not here to tell you to become a trad wife, cook all the time, or always buy in bulk to save money. We've all heard that same old advice before.

On the contrary, keeping my kitchen in a minimalist state for over a decade has been one of the biggest contributions to AJ and me being able to retire early. I think of a Lean Kitchen as one that you are excited to cook in because it's clean, has just what you need without rummaging, and doesn't require a ton of upkeep.

A study by Cornell University researchers found that the average person makes approximately 35,000 remotely conscious decisions a day. And while this number sounds bonkers, the researchers showed that we make around 226 decisions each day on food alone! Think about the last time you went to a restaurant. *Should I order a drink? What drink should I get? Should I get an appetizer? Am I trying to be healthy today? Should we share or should I get my own?* See where I'm going with this? We haven't even hit the main course! When we have to make choice after choice, it's no wonder our mental energy and willpower are totally depleted.

I quote this study often when I teach financial education because I surmised a basic premise: If you can make fewer choices a day, you can spend more brain power making higher-quality and tougher choices in your finances. At first, I didn't know where to start on reducing the potential 35,000 decisions. But I decided that if I could get down to making only 20% of the food decisions per day (good, old-fashioned World Peas rule coming back again), then I could use the brain power I would have spent on the other 80% toward something more pressing than food.

So, by maintaining the habit of a Lean Kitchen, you can significantly impact your financial health and your sanity. Let's learn what a Lean Kitchen is and delve into my personal strategies, which have helped me maintain this habit for over a decade.

BUT I LOVE FOOD!

Now, I know some of you may be thinking, *But, Bernadette—food is life!* And I hear you; I'm Asian after all. We have a saying, "Camera eats first," meaning we love to document all the cool kinds of food we eat. But if you think about how many meals you'll eat in a lifetime, do you really need to make it the best meal ever every single time? If the average person in the US lives to be about seventy-eight years old and they eat 3 meals a day, that's roughly 85,468 meals in a lifetime! Not every meal you have has to be Instagram-worthy or the most amazing meal possible. Eating for health and wealth can mean that your meals aren't always fancy.

Stock Your Lean Kitchen Using the Zero-Hero Strategy

Keeping a Lean Kitchen is the perfect habit to stack with your Zero-Hero Strategy by incorporating it into your monthly budgeting routine. Just as you account for every dollar in the Zero-Hero Strategy, you can have a plan for every food item in your kitchen to be sure it's used wisely. During your budgeting time, take inventory of what you already have stored in your refrigerator, on your kitchen counters, and in your pantry. This not only prevents impulse purchases but also ensures that every ingredient serves a purpose and you just buy what you need.

AJ being an operations expert and me with my MBA, we both unconsciously applied the inventory management principle of "first in, first out" (FIFO) to our kitchen, ensuring that older products are eaten before newer ones. The FIFO approach jives with our Asian tendencies to minimize food waste and maximize value. I am diligent about organizing my pantry and refrigerator to prioritize older items at the front.

I also batch cook and freeze portions for future use once a month if I've noticed any ingredients that have been sitting around for a while. I had always thought about my freezer for obvious things like meats and packaged frozen items, but now I freeze bagels, cookies, spices, and other things that in the past I just forced myself to eat faster instead of spreading out. I have a habit of buying pan de sal, a Filipino bread, every time I visit my family in Las Vegas because I can't get it locally in North Carolina. It turns out it freezes really well, and I get to have it as a treat for a few weeks instead of trying to finish it quickly.

By utilizing ingredients to their fullest potential, you can mirror the principles of the Zero-Hero Strategy to create a zen and efficient kitchen!

Opt for Fresh Foods over Nonperishable Bulk

While buying in bulk may seem cost-effective, it often leads to unnecessary expenditures and waste in the long run. In my experience, I've learned that bulk buying only starts to make financial sense for families of five or more. I got my first Costco membership recently, and while I like buying certain items there, I've found that I'm buying more random things (like giant plushies and desserts) than had I just gone to a regular grocery store.

In a Lean Kitchen, prioritizing freshness over bulk ensures that you only buy what you need, when you need it. Fresh ingredients not only taste better but are generally healthier than their bulk-packaged counterparts. Even better, buying fresh once a week allows for greater flexibility in meal planning. AJ and I enjoy going to our local international grocery store once a week and challenge ourselves to try a new protein source or produce than we did the previous week. Yes, I'm the woman who's blocking the chicken section, looking for the cheapest pack of chicken thighs to save an extra 23 cents. When it comes to grocery shopping, I've found that hunting for the best deals on meat can significantly impact your budget.

For example, I absolutely love eating Korean barbecue, but beef short ribs can be expensive. At my local international grocery store, the traditional cut is $11.99 per pound. But I buy the end cuts, which are only $7.99 per pound. They aren't as pretty but actually have fewer bones, and they get cut up into pieces when you cook them anyway. By comparing prices per pound and opting for cuts on sale or discounted packages, you can save a substantial amount over time.

If you eat the same thing every day, you're not challenging your gut microbiome, which is essential for immunity and proper nutrition absorption, and you're not getting the variety of nutrients you need. Also, I just get bored of eating the same meals over and over again.

Rather than being constrained by large quantities of the same products, you have the freedom to experiment with diverse recipes and flavors. This not only keeps meals exciting but also reduces the likelihood of food fatigue, where repetitive meals become uninspiring and you then feel the urge to order in on a whim, costing you more money.

We buy cooked rotisserie chicken for $8.99 at the beginning of the week, but we'll turn it into different meals throughout the week by adding in different carbs, spices, and vegetables. The rotisserie chicken turns into tacos, stir-fried rice, chicken salad sandwiches, chicken noodle soup, and spring rolls with that one convenient purchase!

The habit we've adopted from our love of Korean culture is the idea of "banchan." Banchan are the assortment of small side dishes served alongside a main course in Korean meals. These side dishes include yummy items like kimchi (fermented vegetables), namul (seasoned vegetables), pickled vegetables, fish cakes, tofu, and other small dishes.

We often buy prepared banchan from our Asian grocery store, but I'll also make my own American versions, like cucumber salad, creamed corn, and potato salad, that will last a few days in the fridge and cost only a few dollars to make for a week's worth of sides. Having multiple side dishes ready to go adds diversity of flavors, textures, and colors to the meals and saves so much time cooking.

Cut Down the Kitchen Clutter

A cluttered kitchen not only impedes efficiency but also leads to overspending. Unused gadgets, expired ingredients, and duplicate items clutter valuable space. Friends and family who come over to our place always comment how clean our kitchen is and how uncluttered our refrigerator is. My Filipino mom always had a packed kitchen, whether it was leftovers in the fridge, meats in the freezer, pots and pans she'd collected over the years, or her ever-growing collection of plates and serving ware for each season. I think doing the opposite in my own home is my form of rebellion.

Regardless of my personal preferences, the fact is that you don't need a ton of kitchen gadgets to cook great meals.

The tools that we use most frequently are:

- An air fryer, replacing a toaster and used as an oven and for frying.
- A pot for boiling pasta, noodles, and soups.
- A couple of different-sized pans.
- A wok—we use this the most frequently.
- A bamboo steamer that fits nicely on top of the wok.
- A combo rice cooker/slow cooker because what Asian household doesn't have rice?!

Your list might look different, of course. A way that I've cut down on kitchen appliances is to put all the ones that I don't use that often in the same cabinet, and if after six months I haven't gone to reach for them, I donate them. Consider storing your less-frequently-used items in the same place, and go there first for the Declutter-the-Date challenge!

REMEMBER THE $1 RULE WHEN YOU MAKE KITCHEN PURCHASES

I'm embarrassed to say this, but on our wedding registry, I asked for a waffle maker, a panini press, a coffee maker, and a bunch of other gadgets that have not survived through our subsequent moves. Before you buy anything for your kitchen, ask yourself if the product will meet the $1 Rule. If not, you probably don't need it.

Another move AJ and I made was to stop keeping free cups we get from events. We also stopped collecting coffee mugs, and we don't buy into the next water bottle craze. We do keep a matching set of eight reusable storage containers that we replace once a year and that make our refrigerator look neat and organized. Once a month, I reorganize my kitchen to put everything back in the place it should be, because God knows we never put things back in the same places after taking them out of the dishwasher.

The one totally unnecessary kitchen item we have is a little sushi train, because AJ and I secretly love going to those conveyor-belt sushi restaurants. I thought I could at least put all my banchan on it. It was $25, and our guests always get a kick out of it when we put it on the dining room table. So, you don't have to be crazy strict about this. Making the kitchen and eating at home fun can make all the difference.

The major game changer for us in saving money was one simple switch: eating from smaller plates and bowls. We have the habit of finishing what's on our plates (thanks, Asian parents), and so smaller plates mean we eat a lot less. Normal dinner plates are 10 or 12 inches, but we eat from 7.5-inch plates. And our bowls are smaller Asian rice bowls rather than the larger cereal bowls that we see in other American households. Our non-Asian friends who we've invited over for meals have commented how small our plates are, but over time they've shared that they've switched their habit over to smaller plates too!

This habit has saved us a ton of money because we're eating much less overall. Our weekly grocery budget is now around $75, when it used to be double that. We've been able to downsize to a smaller kitchen, and we only buy new kitchen gadgets when one needs replacing, instead of collecting more clutter. This has made it more enjoyable to cook at home and has saved us thousands of dollars in food expenses over the last few years.

RICH REFLECTIONS

Reflect on your current kitchen setup. What areas feel cluttered or inefficient and why? How does simplifying your kitchen align with your overall lifestyle goals and values?

Think about your cooking habits and meal planning routines. How could adopting a lean approach to ingredients and meal prep enhance your culinary experience?

How can you cultivate a more intentional approach to purchasing, using, and storing food and kitchen items?

Imagine inviting guests into your Lean Kitchen. How do you envision their reactions and interactions with the space? How does the environment reflect your values and priorities?

How might simplifying your food budget influence other areas of your life, such as relationships and personal growth?

THE FINE DINING ALLOWANCE:
How Dining Out Pays Dividends

There's a certain financial expert who says if you have debt, you shouldn't be seeing the inside of a restaurant unless you are working there. That mandate just never jived with me. To me, dining out one to three times a week can be a strategic component of maintaining a Lean Kitchen and a financial independence plan that is realistic in the modern world where parents are working full-time and individuals are experiencing the highest rate of loneliness in history. When I say "fine dining," I don't mean going out to expensive steakhouses with white linen tablecloths. I mean fine, as in stop feeling guilty about eating out! It's fine to want to make eating out a part of your life if you enjoy it!

While cooking at home is generally more cost-effective, the habit of a Fine Dining Allowance can be great for both your life and your money goals. As I've seen while working with many modern women who are balancing career, life, and family, eating out can become a strategic way to save time and energy if you're too busy to cook or just don't enjoy it. Because eating out is such a common part of life as a busy professional, I wanted to find ways to incorporate this into financial planning in a fun and guilt-free way. Beyond that, I would even argue that eating out can potentially save you money, if you are doing it intentionally and watching out for your portions. AJ and I are awesome at hunting for happy hour specials and low-cost fast-casual food options that often come out cheaper than if we were to cook at home!

Eating out three times out of twenty-one meals a week won't be detrimental. But let me be clear that this is not a green light for laziness and mindless eating. Ordering on DoorDash daily is not what this habit is about. Depending on take-out caffeine instead of quality sleep is not it either. Consuming fast food that you know will make you feel like crap later is...well, you get the picture. The headline here is that eating out is not only acceptable but encouraged as long as you are spending and consuming intentionally while doing it.

CHECK THE PRICES ON MENUS

I'm proud to say that I've reached a new comfort level in my finances such that I do order the extra guac. But no matter how much I earn or keep, I don't think I'll ever kick the habit of reading the menu right to left—meaning I do care about how much a dish costs before I order it. However, you may notice that many eateries strategically place higher-priced items at the beginning of the menu to catch your attention. If you see a menu like that, read it from bottom to the top so you'll first encounter the more affordable options. That way, you can make budget-conscious choices without feeling tempted by more premium dishes, and you can enjoy a meal just as nicely without a bigger price tag.

How a Fine Dining Allowance Can Be Financially Smart

There are four reasons why you can consider this habit an important part of your lifestyle and financial plan, and they conveniently all start with the letter "C": culture, conscious health choices, conserving energy, and connection. The CRUSH plan is all about financial independence that fits with and supports your interests. For most of us, that includes going out to eat pretty regularly—whether because we're too tired to cook, we want to try a new food, or we want to meet up with friends. So rather than pretend that's not going to happen, I'd rather face it head-on and teach you how to incorporate it into your budget in a smart way.

Culture

One reason I think dining out should be part of your financial plan is that it can help you connect to and experience specific cultures—whether it's your own or one that's new to you! I don't know about y'all, but one of the main reasons I love to travel is to eat all the cuisines. As a Filipino American who doesn't speak the language of my ancestors and who's only been to the Philippines once, food is one of the few connections I have to my family's heritage. In my current hometown of Charlotte, North

Carolina, there is only one Filipino restaurant and it's more than an hour-long drive away. So when I visit cities like Las Vegas or Los Angeles, you will likely find me visiting the local Filipino bakeries and restaurants, not only to support my fellow Filipinos but because the food feels like home to me.

AJ and I are obsessed with Korean pop music and dramas, popularly referred to as K-Pop and K-dramas, so when there was a tour in South Korea hosted by Noona's Noonchi founder Jeanie Chang, we jumped at the chance. Aside from getting to see our favorite drama shooting locations, the best part of the tour was sharing a variety of Korean meals with our tour mates every day. From Korean fried chicken to street food to making our own bibimbap, it was so fun to share those meals with other Americans who were trying them for the first time. It's what inspired us to incorporate banchan into our Lean Kitchen!

Conscious Health Choices

Eating out can actually be just as healthy as dining at home if you choose wisely. Nowadays, there are so many great healthy dining options that accommodate almost any diet you can think of. That's another reason I want to be sure it can fit into your lifestyle and financial plan. I have a ton of allergies, including shellfish, peanuts, tree nuts, and even soy. (Yes, I'm an Asian who's allergic to soy—it's the universe's little trick on me.) It used to be hard for me to find places to eat that were sensitive to these allergens, but now so many places have easy signage, and staff members are trained to at least ask about the allergens before serving.

I will say that if you have a bland or mostly American palate, then I would agree that eating healthy while dining out can be a challenge. There are plenty of healthy options in other cultural cuisines including Latin, Asian, and Mediterranean. The key to staying within both your financial and calorie budgets is to be conscious of portions. Portion sizes in the US are generally larger than in the rest of the world. It's clearly a culture of "more is better" rather than quality.

Another way to save money is to challenge yourself to see if you can make two or three meals out of your dining-out dishes. I've found that most meals served in American restaurants can equate to three filling portions for AJ and me based on how we eat, so we've gotten used to splitting dishes and taking leftovers home for lunch the next day. One of our favorite Mediterranean restaurants serves huge, heaping grain bowls with tons of vegetables and protein for around $15. We can make three meals out of a serving, coming out to $5 per meal—way less expensive and way tastier than if we were to try and replicate the same dish at home.

Conserving Energy

I'm guilty of watching videos on social media of moms making beautiful meals for their families, but those meals still take a lot of time! While I am a fan of meal prepping, some people don't have the time and energy for all that chopping, cooking, and dishes. Oh, the dishes! For a lot of my clients, dining out is more about conserving energy than saving money, but that's still a great reason to fit it into your budget. If you're a high-earning professional, it may actually make more economical sense to have someone else cook for you, so you can use your precious energy elsewhere.

THERE'S NO SHAME IN FEEDING KIDS TAKEOUT

If you're a busy parent, I will remind you that you are not a bad parent if you don't home cook every meal for your kids. I hate the advice to parents to cook at home for their kids, because chances are it's moms who will take on that responsibility, and many of my CRUSH Bootcamp moms are breadwinners yet are still expected to maintain homes as though they don't work full-time. Maybe it makes sense for you to order that pizza in so you can enjoy more time interacting with your kids than standing over the oven.

I once worked for a CEO who ate a plain chicken breast and salad every day for lunch. No matter where we went out to eat, he would order the exact same thing. At first I thought, *Wow, he is super weird.* But as I observed him, I realized that he was making CEO-level decisions every day, working out consistently to the point of competing in bodybuilding competitions, and being the breadwinner for his extended family, including his sister and parents. Bro also had courtside NBA seats and multiple residences, so I promise you he was not suffering from eating that chicken breast every day.

And while I do believe everyone can cook to some degree, it's a skill, and therefore not everyone will be great at it! Have you ever met someone who just can't cook well no matter how hard they try? I have, and for those people, it might be healthier to put a line item in their budget for dining out than to rely on ramen and plain rice at home.

Connection

In my opinion, dining out is one of the best ways to foster social connections and relaxation, enhancing your overall emotional well-being. As I said, all takeout is not created equal. Meals bought thoughtlessly and out of laziness aren't the same as meals you're eating and sharing with friends and family. I've always thought that food tastes better when in good company. Coffee you buy just to get through your day is different from coffee where you treat a friend to catch up after not seeing each other for a while. There's no shame in buying either, but the latter pays dividends that feed your soul.

Despite the benefits, dining out can get pricey if you don't have an intentional plan around it. I encourage the CRUSH Bootcamp to incorporate eating out one to three times a week, with at least one of those meals having the purpose of reconnecting with someone they care about. To keep dining-out costs down, you can:

- Take advantage of happy hour deals instead of the full-price menu
- Try street food rather than a fancy restaurant from a country you hope to visit together someday
- Swap dinner dates for breakfast dates, which are more affordable
- Grab some ice cream and take a walk together
- Support a sandwich shop and take them for a picnic in the park

Connection is a very important part of being a happy human. Dining out has been an important way for me to share in the life experiences of my closest friends. One of my best friends, Aiko, is half-Japanese, and her parents now live in Japan. She visits Japan frequently to see them. So, whenever she offers to take me to a new Japanese restaurant in New York where she lives, I always say yes, because I know she will show me the good stuff! It always precipitates conversations about her past travels and how she grew up with a Japanese father. I treasure learning those things about her even though we've known each other for over two decades.

That being said, I reserve dining out for friends who I genuinely love spending time with—the kinds of friends who I can treat for dinner and know that they will get me back the next time around. I've also pretty much stopped drinking alcohol altogether, not only because $20 cocktails aren't fun to pay for but because the friendships I've had based around drinking were fake at worst and shallow at best. The best conversations I've ever had over meals have always been sober and authentic.

The bottom line is this—eating has become a mindless activity for many of us in an increasingly digital world. I encourage you to use a Fine Dining Allowance as a way to be mindful with your money. By incorporating dining experiences into your monthly budgeting strategy, you can indulge in culinary outings without compromising your financial goals.

RICH REFLECTIONS

Consider your dining-out habits. How often do you eat out with loved ones, and how does it align with your financial goals?

Reflect on the impact of dining out on your relationships with loved ones. How does sharing a meal together contribute to your bond, and how can you make those moments more intentional?

Explore alternative dining options that offer opportunities for connection without breaking the bank, such as picnics in the park or cooking together at home. What are ten ideas you can bank for your Fine Dining Allowance?

Consider the role of planning and preparation in making dining-out experiences more intentional. How can you proactively plan outings with loved ones to ensure they align with your financial goals?

Explore the concept of quality over quantity when dining out with loved ones. Who are the next five people you want to prioritize meaningful experiences and connections with and why?

THE LITTLE LUXURIES LOOP:
Reward Yourself with 5% Cash Back

Do you love collecting credit card points? According to research, people love using credit cards and even feel the fear of missing out on rewards and point programs. The reality is those rewards are designed to encourage more spending, which can contradict your efforts to save money and pay down debt. But let's be real—collecting points *is* fun! It feels like free money! So, this next habit borrows the credit card companies' genius strategy but allows you to pay yourself back in little luxuries.

Keeping Yourself Motivated As You Pay Off Debt

While many debt-free proponents say you must cut out every unnecessary expense, I promise you that long-term deprivation will make your personal finances feel like drudgery. I don't know about y'all, but if I don't get any sort of short-term gratification while working on a hard goal, I'll just quit. While I was paying off my student loans, the first few thousand dollars were relatively easy to tackle, but I soon hit a plateau and was really close to giving up. To try to keep myself motivated, I implemented my own 5% cash back habit to treat myself for milestones I made along a longer debt payoff goal.

If you have a large amount of debt—say $100,000 in student loans, like many millennials do—it can feel like climbing a mountain when you can't even see the top. The point of this habit is to take that big, lofty number (that mountain) and break it down into smaller, more manageable chunks (hills).

Here's the fun part! Once you hit each smaller milestone, promise to pay yourself back 5% to treat yourself for hitting your goal. For example, you could pay off $1,000 of debt at a time and give yourself a $50 treat, or you could go for $10,000 increments and treat yourself to $500 each time. Yes, sis! It's okay to treat yourself while you have debt—you are allowed to have some fun!

START SIMPLE AND PAIR THIS HABIT WITH YOUR FINE DINING ALLOWANCE!

If you're not sure what reward you might want, buy yourself a gift card and use it at your favorite local eatery until the card runs out. For example, you can treat yourself to several coffees or your favorite dessert. A $50 gift card for my favorite local bakery would get me almost ten tres leches cakes! Because we both have a sweet tooth, AJ and I have turned it into a fun challenge to use our little luxuries money to try a new local bakery each time! From Latin to Korean bakeries, it's been a great way to reward ourselves, explore our city, and satisfy our cravings.

What Does Luxury Mean to You?

Here's an unfortunate side effect I've learned that people experience when they have financial anxiety: They don't even know what luxury means to them. The American vision of luxury is often unrealistic and capitalistic and looks like a 1990s rap video: yachts and champagne and designer clothes. But part of a meaningful financial independence plan is deciding what luxury looks like for *you*.

The simple definition of luxury is something that adds pleasure or comfort to your life but isn't absolutely necessary. Luxury doesn't have to mean expensive, but it does have to be something that makes you smile or feel warm and fuzzy inside. As you plan your treats, first think about what rewards would be meaningful to you.

The importance here is that you use that money toward what best represents a little luxury to you. Please don't use it to pay an extra bill or buy cleaning products. Unless, of course, you are one of those weird people who actually enjoy cleaning their homes and find that to be a luxury—then more power to you!

Marie Paid Off $50,000 of Debt and Now Helps Other Women Find Luxury!

Marie is a proud first-generation Asian American woman who is deeply passionate about helping other women have better lives so that they, in turn, can go be badasses and make the world a better place—down with the patriarchy! Marie helps women create beautiful homes that reflect their very best selves, allowing them joyful places to recharge so they can go fix the world. Marie joined the CRUSH Bootcamp as an early member and has been one of the most inspirational people in my life, personally and professionally.

Marie shared, "I have so appreciated your content and offerings over the last several years. Following your principles, I have paid off over $50,000 of credit card debt, quit my job, and launched a luxury residential interior design business in Charlotte, North Carolina. Thanks to you, in my first two years I have generated over a million dollars in revenue and am doing it debt-free!"

Marie was able to do all this because she is amazing, but also she finally learned how to stick to a budget that allowed her to splurge on little luxuries instead of feeling restricted. I've personally witnessed her use her little luxuries allowance as a fellow K-pop fan to take her best friend and daughter Emma to K-pop concerts and to take their first trip to Seoul, South Korea, together. I've loved witnessing Marie's growth from guilty shopper to confident consumer and world traveler, and she's also become one of my favorite humans on earth!

Schedule Your 5% Cash Shopping Splurges

I have a hard time with male-dominated personal finance advice because it often categorizes shopping as frivolous, when women drive 70 to 80% of all consumer-purchasing decisions. That's not to say that all shopping habits are justified—I'm absolutely guilty of shopping as a form of coping with stress, grief, or anxiety, even as a money coach. I'd love to say I kicked that habit, but truthfully, it's hard to let go of a habit that I actually enjoy.

Rather than restricting myself from shopping, I now schedule a day once a month where I'm "allowed" to shop with my little luxuries money. That might mean a walk around the mall or carving out time to browse my favorite brands. I schedule my shopping time for Thursday afternoons, after my toughest and longest workdays. It's also great to have a weekday during which I can decompress and have a little mindless fun and not have to fight the weekend crowds.

This plan may seem like it encourages me to spend more, but instead it's actually curbed my impulses to shop the other days of the month. Even if I have a tough day on a Tuesday, my other long workday, I give myself permission to blow off that steam on that scheduled Thursday rather than go on the impulse immediately.

It's nice knowing I have a day to look forward to, and surprisingly, it has removed the lifestyle creep of many small purchases. My shopping is now more intentional, with purchases happening all on the same day versus scattered throughout the month. This has helped me see my purchases relative to one another and keep them squarely within my Revive budget.

But to me, even more rewarding than anything I can buy at the mall or even sweets is to treat myself to larger experiences like concert tickets, hobbies, or throwing a little celebration each time. A client of mine involved her two kids in the process and drew a big thermometer in their living room. Whenever they paid off $1,000 of debt, the whole family went out for pizza. Soon, the kids were asking how they could help pay down more debt—it was so cute!

Your little luxury could be fishing, hiking, camping, or snowboarding. It doesn't have to be something traditionally luxurious! Reframing luxury to mean *time* well spent more than *money* well spent can excite you even more to break down your big money goals and hit those milestones, because you can make a new memory each time.

DON'T FORGET TO STACK YOUR HABITS!

This habit meshes with the Three Life Buckets and Zero-Hero Strategy habits. By planning for that luxury line item, you can keep the rest of your budget on track while rewarding yourself for the hard work you've done in paying down your debt. You can also stack this habit with your monthly budget to plan your splurge days close to the days you know you'll be stressed, to help prevent impulse purchases and plan ahead!

Invest in Little Luxuries by Matching Your Future Self

If you don't have any debt to attach the 5% cash back rule to, you can still break down other money goals and treat not only yourself but your future self too! When I became debt-free, it was arguably just as hard to stay debt-free as it had been to pay down my debt. I suddenly felt like I could afford more, even though I still wasn't saving enough for retirement. Before I knew it, I was going back to my old shopping habits and shoe collecting, which I had curtailed in order to pay off student loans.

I started implementing the Little Luxuries Loop habit again when I observed how many of my money-coaching clients contributed to their 401(k)s rather blindly because they wanted to get the "free money" in employer matching, even when they were struggling to pay their everyday bills. I did it in a different way: I matched the money I spent on luxury line items with a donation of the same amount to my 401(k)—in other words, to my future self.

In the United States, a 401(k) match is money contributed by your employer to your 401(k) retirement account—it's a great benefit that some companies offer. For each dollar you save in your 401(k), your employer will match your contribution, up to a certain percentage of your salary.

Nowadays, I don't deprive myself of buying clothes that I want—as long as I am also willing to invest at the same rate that I shop. For example, if I spend $200 on a jacket that I really wanted to buy, I can buy it and also contribute $200 into my 401(k) account. Implementing this connection between now and later helps you really evaluate how badly you want to buy something, knowing it will essentially cost you twice as much in your budget.

I used to view it as a way to give myself spending boundaries, but recently I've put a more positive spin on it thanks to the CRUSH Bootcamp: When you buy something for your current self, you can also choose to match your future self with a treat too.

Giving yourself permission to enjoy a little luxury and knowing that you can still succeed financially will make staying within a budget more manageable. Keep the guilt out of shopping by rewarding yourself along the way, not just at the goal post. You may not hit your smaller milestones the way you want every time, which means that you might not get your little luxury. But that also means that when you do get that treat, it's even more meaningful!

RICH REFLECTIONS

Describe what luxury means to you personally. How do you differentiate between extravagant, materialistic luxury and the simple pleasures that add joy and comfort to your life?

Reflect on the intersection of short-term gratification and long-term financial goals. How do you balance the need for immediate rewards with the patience required for achieving larger financial milestones?

Reflect on your relationship with credit card points and rewards. How can you replicate that same gratification without necessarily spending more?

How could setting aside specific times for indulgence impact your spending habits and overall financial well-being?

What little luxuries would you want to treat your future self to ten years from now? Imagine how your future self would feel. What would you say to her?

7

Heal Your Money Wounds

The last step of CRUSH is the hardest, and it's something I am on a life-long journey to master—healing money wounds. When I say "money wounds," I'm talking about the emotional or psychological scars that we carry from our experiences with money, finances, and financial decisions. These wounds can stem from childhood upbringing, societal influences, personal experiences, and significant life events. Money wounds can manifest in different ways and may include feelings of shame, guilt, fear, inadequacy, or unworthiness related to money and wealth. These feelings can sometimes appear when you least expect them.

I sometimes think of these money wounds in relation to a common skin condition I have called eczema. Basically, it's when your skin gets all red, itchy, and super irritated. The causes are a combo of genetics, environmental factors, and your immune system acting up. Eczema can show up anywhere on your body, but it's most common on your hands, arms, elbows, knees, and face—and let me tell you, it's not at all subtle. When I was a child, I never went swimming because I was embarrassed by all the flaky patches on my body. As an adult, I had the CEO of my company ask me what was wrong with my face during a meeting. I've felt embarrassed, ashamed, and ugly many times in my life.

Managing my eczema since childhood has taken some trial and error to figure out what will tame it. Some folks find relief with moisturizers, while others swear by special creams or ointments and avoid triggers like certain soaps, fabrics, or even stress (yep, stress can totally mess with your skin). I've tried them all.

Working through money wounds, for me, has been very much like managing my skin condition. Scratching only makes my eczema worse (even though it feels so freaking good)—I need to stop aggravating the patches. Money wounds are the same—the more you "scratch" them, or continue them, the more they distract you from your everyday life and the less likely they are to heal. And for both my eczema and money wounds, I realized I was relying too much on outside remedies when what I really needed to do was address the internal stresses, not just the external symptoms.

Have you felt any of these money wounds before?

- **Financial trauma:** Past financial losses, getting laid off, or money hardships that leave lasting scars
- **Scarcity mindset:** Feeling a constant fear of not having enough money, even when you're okay
- **Overspending:** Using retail therapy as a coping mechanism for emotional distress or to fill a void
- **Fear of success:** Feeling afraid of the responsibilities and expectations that come with wealth
- **Financial dependence:** Overly relying on others or feeling trapped in financial relationships
- **Inherited beliefs:** Internalizing negative attitudes about money that were passed down to you
- **Comparison and envy:** Constantly comparing your financial situation to others' and feeling inadequate

By being honest and healing these emotional wounds, you can develop healthier habits around money, leading you to feel joy in your journey, not just stress! I'm wary of money coaching that becomes unlicensed therapy, so we won't delve *too* deeply here. Fully addressing money wounds often involves introspection, self-awareness, and seeking support from trusted individuals, financial experts, and therapists. Let's simply start to unearth and recognize any underlying sentiments that could be holding you back from financial independence and happiness. In this last part of CRUSH, I'll share five money habits that can kick you off in the right direction of managing your money and emotions around your money goals.

THE UNSUBSCRIBE BUTTON:
Reclaim Your Income

For this habit, you're going to reframe any monthly payments as basically subscriptions that got you to buy things for more than they're worth. Take a moment now to write a list of all the "subscriptions" you currently have. These are the ones that are more obvious:

- Software, such as phone apps, productivity services, and licenses, like Microsoft Office
- Delivery services, such as meal subscriptions, clothing boxes, and recurring Amazon orders (for example, I had laundry detergent coming every month to the point I had too much)
- Memberships, like fitness memberships, time-shares, social clubs, online learning platforms, and digital publications
- Streaming services, including video content like Netflix as well as audio content like Spotify

Now, don't hop aboard the guilt train—that's not the point of me asking you to evaluate this. The habit I'm asking you to cultivate is to utilize the Unsubscribe Button more often than you use the subscribe one. And if you're going to subscribe, do so with greater intention than you have ever before. In particular, unsubscribe from any service that:

- You wouldn't pay the full price for if you had the money. For example, a streaming service might be $9.99 a month, but for a year, that's $120. Ask yourself if that $120 is worth it to you.
- Is going underutilized or unused—remember, if you cancel and realize you miss it, you can always rejoin later.
- Isn't of the best quality you can expect as a customer. If their customer service sucks, or their content can be found elsewhere, consider a higher-quality service, even if it means it's more expensive.

STOP GIVING SOMEONE ELSE EASY PASSIVE INCOME

One of the most common questions I get from CRUSH Bootcamp members is: "How do I make passive income?" And my first response is always: "Stop being someone else's passive income first." I know, that stung a little bit. Have you ever thought about the idea that the interest you pay on any debt is making someone else rich by being their passive income stream?

- **A mortgage** is a subscription to a home that can cost you hundreds of thousands of dollars more than the home value in the form of interest—the bank just had to complete one set of paperwork to get it from you.
- **A car payment or lease** is a monthly subscription that's more profitable for the car company than you owning it outright—the car company just had to sell you that one car to get thousands in passive income.
- **Premium credit cards** are a subscription for perks that cost the company pennies on the dollar to offer you, all the while charging you 20% or more in interest—returns you would never get as an average stock investor.

Obviously, there are certain "subscriptions" that you realistically can't avoid paying for. You need to keep subscribing to your electricity and Internet and phone bills if you want to participate in modern society. But less vital subscriptions have taken over our finances, and it's time to claim our budgets back. Now, in your defense, this is not a "you" problem—marketing experts figured out that most people are willing to pay big amounts of money in smaller chunks for the sake of convenience.

Unsubscribe from Five Social Media Accounts and Email Subscriptions That Cue You to Spend Money

In researching for this book, I found that there wasn't a lot of tangible advice on how to manage social media and its impact on our money management skills. There was especially not much discussion on social media's role in exacerbating our money wounds. I am in that millennial generation that remembers childhood before there was social media and after. Specifically, I went to Boston University, one of the early universities to have *Facebook* back when Mark Zuckerberg wasn't a household name, and it was a social network rather than social media. The good old days when I was only bombarded by pictures of my ex-boyfriends instead of ads!

I remember specifically thinking that if I had fewer than a thousand friends, I would be a loser, and if I didn't post cool song lyrics or pictures of me partying (pictures I now regret exist), people would think I was a total nerd. I know that sounds stupid, but it's true. I'd love to say I was confident and secure and all the girl-boss things I should be saying as a personal finance expert, but I was a run-of-the-mill millennial young adult who just wanted to belong. And it's that desperate need to feel seen and loved and heard that drives many of our spending habits.

But unlike generations past, you don't have to go very far to measure yourself against the success of the other people around you. You can test your sense of self-worth minute by minute, hour by hour...it's readily accessible twenty-four seven and sitting in your pocket. As of 2023, *Forbes Advisor* estimated 4.9 billion people globally use social media, so it's easy to feel alone if you're trying to have healthier social media habits.

It might seem like social media is free and harmless, but it's costing us more than we think. According to a 2023 Bankrate survey, 48% of social media users reported that platforms such as Instagram and TikTok led them to make an impulse purchase, and 68% of those buyers regretted their decision.

Researchers at the MIT Sloan School of Management found a "significant link" between access to Facebook and more anxiety and depression among college students. If you're not prepared to shut down total access, deciding to "mute" five social media accounts is a small step that can be a game changer for your financial well-being. Open your social media app and identify at least five accounts you follow that often trigger impulses to spend money, whether they suggest you buy sponsored products, promote experiences that are not in your budget, or make you feel less satisfied with what you already have.

Previously, you had to purposefully unfollow an account, risking a potentially awkward interaction if you knew the person in real life. Now you can use mute options on social media platforms to still follow those accounts but not have them show up in your feed. If you want to see what those people are up to, you'll have to make a conscious effort to visit their pages.

I TRADED STREAMING FOR REAL-LIFE EXPERIENCES

By now you know that I am absolutely obsessed with Korean content, from following K-pop idol groups to watching variety shows and dramas. The possible subscriptions I could have from fan club memberships to streaming services could be hundreds of dollars a month. I don't have a Netflix account, despite the plethora of content there. Instead, I have only one entertainment subscription, which is specifically dedicated to Asian entertainment shows, and it costs $9.99 per month. Now when I go to live concerts and entertainment shows, they feel even more special than if I had just watched the replays on video.

I took the money I would have spent on the combination of Spotify, YouTube Premium, Hulu, and Netflix (all of which I've had in the past) and decided to allocate those funds toward an $80 monthly membership to my local yoga studio instead. I now go to yoga three to five times a week, and that subscription has not only helped me get stronger but also get better sleep as opposed to staying up all night watching TV like I used to.

The bottom line of this habit is this—subscriptions aren't bad as long as you continue them with the intent of using them to their full capacity and as long as they make your time feel more valued, not less. Making the Unsubscribe Button one of your core money habits will not only save you money but also the time to focus on living in the real world.

Unsubscribe (Again and Again) from Email Marketing

Habitually unsubscribing from those pesky promotional emails can help you save money in so many ways. The most obvious benefit I've personally experienced is reducing the impulse purchasing. Promotional emails are designed to tempt you into special offers and limited-time deals. But if I don't know about them, I won't be tempted! More importantly, without the constant email reminders of sales, I've improved my ability to exercise delayed gratification, and I rarely shop online nowadays. When I budget, I prioritize spending on essentials rather than budgeting for nonessential items that I saw on a marketing campaign.

But the biggest benefit I get from unsubscribing consistently from marketing emails is reducing the email overload. When I started working in a corporate environment, I got into the habit of completely cleaning out my inbox before I could move on to anything else for the day. But the more offers I signed up for, the more stressful my overflowing inbox became, even if it just took a few clicks to get rid of those emails. Reducing the email clutter has lowered my stress and minimized distractions throughout the day.

Make it a habit to unsubscribe from emails as soon as you realize you don't get any value from them, rather than just deleting them. Most emails have an "unsubscribe" link at the bottom. You can also use email-management tools designed to help you unsubscribe from multiple lists quickly and easily rather than going through them one by one. For example, I love Gmail because I can unsubscribe from emails without going to each of their individual links and also flag senders to go to my junk mail rather than entering my inbox.

Without the constant sales pitches, you become more aware of your spending habits, and you also reduce the likelihood of starting new subscriptions that you'll have to unsubscribe from later!

RICH REFLECTIONS

Do you feel inspired with your social media consumption? What specifically needs to change to start aligning it with your financial-freedom plan?

Have you noticed any patterns of increased anxiety or dissatisfaction after spending time on social platforms? How did you feel?

When have you felt pressure to conform to certain standards regarding material possessions, beauty, or experiences? How has it influenced your subscription choices and your self-worth? Be honest.

Are there specific email subscriptions from retail companies or sales messages that tend to trigger impulsive spending for you? How might unsubscribing from these contribute to better spending habits?

What are three areas in your life you could use more positive influence from (e.g., health, wealth, hobbies)? Name three sources you can find and consume them in a healthier way.

THE SCREENLESS SUNDAY:
Digitally Detox from Constant Comparisons

In addition to preventing expenditures on random stuff you don't need, taking a weekly break from your phone will infinitely improve your odds of success at achieving financial independence. The one habit that I've consistently cultivated to improve this dynamic is called the Screenless Sunday, and it's exactly what it sounds like. I'm excited for you to try it even once, even if it doesn't become one of your regular habits.

The goal of the Screenless Sunday habit is simple—spend the whole day doing anything other than using your phone in order to avoid needless spending. Ideally, that also means you don't look at any television or computer screens, but I'll confess I haven't mastered that yet. There are just too many good Korean dramas to watch, and I will sneak in an episode once in a while! The feeling of not having a phone all day can only be described as pure liberation. It's like my brain can rest and actually live and breathe in the real world.

The Rise of Social Media–Induced Spending

I've started to recommend the Screenless Sunday to many of my clients because it became clear to me that their spending was induced by social media, not by their actual wants or needs. In particular, the constant comparison to what they saw and therefore felt like they needed caused them to blow their budgets without even knowing why.

I bet you know this intuitively, but I'm here to remind you that the portrayals of lifestyles you see on social media, even from your close friends, isn't real. Your friends are showcasing the idealized versions of their lives, whether it be their new gadgets, adventures, or pristine homes. Whether you realize it or not, you will feel the pressure to conform when you see your friends with the latest trends and feel the need to buy them to feel like you belong. Water cups are the perfect example of this! At the time I'm writing this book, ten-year-old girls are begging their moms for

$50 Stanley water bottles. That's a product of social media influencing, not what ten-year-old girls want or need.

I have often been perceived as a social media influencer because I do like to post hobbies and experiences I have, but I am the first to tell you that I despise influencer culture. Most people don't realize that influencers are paid money from brands to make it appear as though those brands' products are life-changing and part of their daily lives. This regular exposure to high-end lifestyles has unfortunately shifted our perception of what's actually "normal" and, by design, created that fear of missing out, or "FOMO," that has become so commonplace.

I hate to admit this, but I have totally fallen for this myself, particularly when seeing others showcasing their purchases. The desire to share and gain approval from my friends absolutely led me to spend more on things that were "shareworthy" rather than what I actually wanted or needed. For me it was less of an issue with things like clothes and household goods, but I definitely felt less happy about my home and my car when I saw other people who had nicer ones than mine! Once I started the Screenless Sunday habit, I definitely felt a sense of relief not only in my social media–induced spending but in my incessant need to compare myself to my friends online.

When I began this habit, I used to have AJ hide my phone from me and promise not to give it back, no matter how much I pestered him. I once watched a television show where people locked their phones in a clear safe with a timer and couldn't use the phone until the timer was up—it's wild how addicted we are to our phones. But now I simply put my phone into my car's glove compartment on Saturday nights and do my best to leave it there until Monday morning.

Even if you logistically can't go all in on a completely Screenless Sunday, try cultivating a habit of a different day or time block each week when you can let go of the phone and give your social anxiety time to heal. If you can't do it every week, start with trying it once a month or even once a quarter. The average American adult spends four to five hours a day on their phone—and many of those hours explicitly or implicitly influence your money choices to favor consumerism over freedom. I'm embarrassed to say, but I've had days when I was on my phone for over six hours, and

I felt totally disgusted when I realized that none of it was helpful for my health or wealth.

LET YOUR FAMILY AND FRIENDS CHOOSE SCREENLESS SUNDAYS INSTEAD OF FORCING IT

At first, I chose to do this habit alone—I didn't want to force a habit onto my husband that he wasn't down for. But he's pleasantly agreed to do it with me more often than not, and it's done wonders for our marriage. It turns out without phones, we're forced to entertain ourselves and learn how to be engaging to others...plus, we interact in a more intentional and meaningful way. Chances are, if people around you see the Screenless Sunday habit working well for you, they'll be inspired to try it on their own without your direction.

Use Screenless Sundays As a Household Reset

Despite the increase of remote work, women at all levels of the workforce are still far more likely than men to be responsible for more of the caregiving and their family's housework. Even when I was producing more income than my husband, I still felt the majority of the responsibility to keep our home organized and well maintained. I often resented times when our family members asked him about his career advancement but asked me about having kids. You do want to be careful to not let Screenless Sunday just become a day when you do housework nonstop—that's not the main point.

My husband and I do sometimes use Sundays to do our budgets together, but we also use the time to divide our housework and caregiving responsibilities as equitably as possible, with both our work schedules in mind for the upcoming week. And once a quarter, we use one of our Screenless Sundays to put our whole household back to where it should be and consider our Lean Kitchen habit—cleaning out clutter, deep cleaning the nooks and crannies, and taking inventory of what we need for our next grocery purchase.

But when neither of us has the capacity, we outsource tedious tasks that used to burn us out: grocery shopping, laundry, housekeeping, and lawn maintenance. Even though I was raised to think these chores were ones I should do myself, I learned to pay for the chores to get done when I was exhausted rather than pay with my mental health. If you're on the brink of burnout, or are already there, I strongly encourage you to reframe your view of budgeting from a burdensome task to a way of freeing up not just your money but your time and energy to live more than you work. Screenless Sundays are more fun as play days than as chore days!

Take Your Online Interests Offline

A 2023 Meta-Gallup survey found that 24% of people across the world have reported feeling very or fairly lonely. Shifting your online interests into real-life social priorities can be transformative for your finances and your sense of belonging. Instead of aligning my social life with my friends' schedules on Sundays, I now prioritize my online interests—music, comedy, travel, and minimalism—as experiences that can translate into new, meaningful connections.

THE ART OF MEMORY MAKING

One of my favorite Screenless Sundays was when my friends Broderick and Eileen came to visit my husband and me on a whim. They drove two hours to where we were, and when they arrived, we spontaneously signed up to do a Clue-themed escape room, based on one of our favorite childhood board games. That day turned into a whole theme, where we pieced together costumes from our closet and ate chocolate fondue while we stayed in character. It's one of my favorite memories with them, and it wouldn't have happened if we were glued to our phones all day!

For example, instead of just watching music videos on YouTube, I prioritized saving up for a live concert with my best friend. I opted to take a live improv class rather than watch funny clips on Instagram. You can start online for inspiration, but take the extra step to plan those new in-person experiences with friends who share similar interests on your screenless days. And if none are available, you can go alone and make an effort to connect with new people—it's daunting at first, but now I look forward to the Sundays when I pick a new spot to scout, because I never know what or who I'll find.

Revisit the Hobbies That Bring You Analog Joy

I know this sounds crazy, but there once was a time when people enjoyed themselves with activities that had zero screens involved. At the time I'm writing this book, there has been a significant revival in hobbies that not only leave the digital world behind but don't cost that much money and stack very nicely with our $1 Rule! Ever since AJ and I instated Screenless Sundays at our home, we've been rekindling the joy we had as kids to:

- Read for pleasure and not just for self-development.
- Play board games (at one point we had over two hundred in AJ's collection).
- Build a plant family—they say dogs are the new kids and plants are the new dogs!
- Listen to music, especially on vinyl—it's amazing to not have to hear ads all the time.
- Practice yoga—I've even gone to back-to-back classes at my local yoga studio, which prohibits technology of any kind.

We've also used our Screenless Sundays to try new restaurants, go ice-skating, make candles and other crafts, and test new recipes. Not to brag, but we're pretty darn cute when we're screenless; you can see how relaxed and peaceful we are when we are focused on the present moment and using our bodies and hands beyond typing on keyboards.

On a recent trip to Boston, we convinced my in-laws and their kids to go screenless for a night. They were grumpy about it at first, but by the end of the night, I had gotten to spend quality time with my nephew playing piano, cooked a vegan dinner for the whole family with my sister-in-law, and introduced them to a fun game that required nothing other than for us to sit in a circle and pay attention to each other. My nephew hugged me when we left, saying he was going to miss us. That made me feel happier than anything we would have watched on TV together instead.

In an unexpected side effect, taking your online interests offline on Sundays can help you no longer feel pressured to attend social events you're not enthusiastic about. This change has significantly broadened my social circle, introducing me to a diverse range of individuals. It can help you save money by focusing on activities you enjoy rather than collecting more things to buy or going to social gatherings centered around drinking and small talk. We have communities of friends from our dance classes and our love of Korean culture, yoga, board games, and music. Who says you have to have one friend who does it all with you?

Rest Is a Great Idea Too!

And a loving reminder that if you do nothing but rest and be a slug on your Screenless Sunday, that is totally an acceptable way to implement this habit. There are 168 hours in a week—taking 8 hours to take a breath, let your body heal, and collect your thoughts is a wonderful and absolutely worthwhile way to spend your day. I often have a hard time sitting still, and I learned it's harder for me to rest than it is to stay busy. A Screenless Sunday sitting on my porch means I was successful at sitting alone with my own thoughts.

I don't believe that our purpose as humans is to sit in front of screens all day long. Your brain needs a break from the screens, your soul needs time to heal, and your health and wealth deserve some screenless time. It's also been a wonderful way for me to "practice" early retirement, rekindling my former hobbies and helping me get excited for a future that isn't me in front of a computer screen all week! Giving yourself the gift of screenless time will help you stay on track for independence based on what you want, not what you see on your social media feed.

RICH REFLECTIONS

Imagine implementing a designated screenless day or time block each week. What challenges do you anticipate, and how do you plan to overcome them?

What benefits will you gain from this habit in terms of financial independence and personal growth?

How do you currently divide household responsibilities with your partner or family members? Do you feel that these responsibilities are distributed equitably? If not, what changes could be made and done on Screenless Sundays?

Think about your online interests and hobbies. How could you translate these interests into real-life experiences or connections?

Commit to one activity you could pursue offline in the next month that aligns with your financial-freedom goals. What will you do? Who will you invite? What will make it "worth it"?

THE DRAMA DRAIN:
Release Energy Vampires

Ever since I hit my first financial independence milestone, I've been practicing and maintaining the habit of being voraciously protective of my calendar—literally and metaphorically. It's the habit that allows me to work twenty hours a week while still making six figures a year and actually loving the job I have. This habit is called the Drama Drain, and it's the weekly habit of releasing the "energy vampires" that take focus away from your financial independence goals and drain you of the energy you need to feel healthy and wealthy.

When people come to me for financial coaching, they say that the top thing they need is a plan. Then I present them with the exact plan that will allow them to reach financial independence…and they don't do it. What do you think the number one excuse is for that? You guessed right—it's time. What I learned, though, is that most people actually *do* have the time. The problem is they are giving that time away to these energy vampires out of habit or out of obligation without stopping to ask themselves if these energy vampires are worth that precious resource of time.

I live in North Carolina, and there's a Southern saying, "Bless your heart," which I eventually learned is not as sweet as it sounds! What it really means is, "Good for you, now beat it!" So, before you say you don't have time for your financial-freedom plan, it's time to make a habit out of blessing and releasing these energy vampires so you have the time to focus on the financial habits that will change your life.

Tips for Keeping a Drama-Free Calendar

Here are some ideas to consider as you get started looking for spots in your week where you can minimize stress and clear out the drama:

- Spend twenty minutes on Sunday evenings or Monday mornings each week to optimize your schedule for the upcoming week.

Heather Got Her Head Out of Her Butt and Reclaimed Her Energy

Heather is my longest active member. She came to my first ever finance class in February 2020 and we have been together ever since. I met with Heather for her regular coaching meeting after a month of extensive travel and "dropped balls" in her court, and it became clear: The energy vampires had taken over her calendar and finances. As a busy tech executive and the main breadwinner of her family, she let board meetings, client complaints, and her family's wants come before her own needs and her finances.

After a hard heart-to-heart and some pointed conversation about the patterns she was repeating, she exclaimed she would get her head out of her butt (her words, not mine!) and reclaim control of her calendar so she could focus on her finances. She realized that two of her biggest energy vampires were her extensive work travel and the pressure of upkeep of her home.

In our coaching session, she established that going forward, she would set a boundary of one work trip per month at a maximum and only go to meetings that absolutely required her physical presence. She also established that she would delegate the home maintenance to her family members as shared responsibility instead of just taking it on herself.

The amazing thing is, in the week after she chose to release those energy vampires, she finally focused on working on her taxes with her accountant and found $10,000 in savings! It goes to show you that when you release draining activities, you have more brain space to find the big bucks, literally!

- Use an online app, such as Google Calendar, that you can edit quickly and from anywhere. Paper planners are pretty, but they're not efficient in managing a hectic schedule.
- Color code the types of events in your calendar so you can balance what you're doing each week. For example, I code health and exercise as green, social gatherings as purple, client meetings as blue, and nonclient meetings as orange.
- Figure out how you like to arrange events that require different levels of energy from you. For example, you could group similar energies together and, say, stack business meetings on one day if getting into a certain mindset and staying there works for you.

- Use a scheduling tool like Calendly or Acuity to let people know your availability, even for personal time. It shows people you are organized, and I've noticed I get a lot fewer flaky people setting up time with me because they have to be intentional about it.

Decline Meetings That Aren't Worth Your Time

Have you ever sat in a work meeting or social gathering where you thought to yourself, *I feel like I'm wasting my time*? If the answer is yes, and if it's happened on more than one occasion, you have some work to do on your meeting boundaries and when you say yes or no to adding time to your very limited calendar.

Quite simply, I decline a lot of meetings. I won't lie—it's hard sometimes, and I wonder if I'm being a jerk, because, especially as a Filipino woman, I feel the expectation to be likable and available to anyone who asks for my time. But as my business and wealth grew, more and more people asked me for face time, and it just wasn't sustainable without sacrificing my own freedom. Now I'm very strict about declining any personal or professional meeting if that meeting:

- **Doesn't have a clear agenda:** If you don't know why you are going to a meeting, you need to ask specifically, and all parties should agree to the agenda beforehand. Speaking as a former HR professional, don't ever put yourself in a position to be caught off guard, especially at your job.
- **Could have been an email:** This is pretty straightforward but often underutilized. If you can accomplish the agenda with one or two emails, just make them emails. Reserve meeting time for deeper-dive discussions.
- **Is asking to "pick my brain":** This has been the hardest, because I want to help, but I learned that many strangers who request this from me either have no intention of following through on my advice or no intention of ever paying me. I learned to say yes by sharing previous content or offering consulting—for a fee.

- **Is with someone unpleasant:** Life is too short to spend it with jerks or people who don't value your time. If one of these jerks is someone you work with, address their behavior sooner rather than later. If it's once or twice, I give people the benefit of the doubt that they may have had a bad day. Three times or more is a pattern.
- **Is anything less than a "Hell yes!":** I used to go to social gatherings out of obligation, even if I didn't feel comfortable around those people, and I've felt so much more freedom now that I only go when I'm excited to go!

Read those descriptions again. I'm sure you've said yes to at least one of these meetings that really should have been a no. Now, imagine how much further you could be in your finances had you taken all that meeting time and put it toward your budget, or investing, or meeting with a valuable money mentor instead. Money is abundant; time is what's scarce. The catch to having these clear meeting boundaries is that you yourself must practice what we're preaching here.

The Right Way to Use Your Time

In order to build this habit, start changing your mindset to be stricter about what events are worth your time. The Drama Drain means when you initiate meetings, there should be a clear agenda. One of my favorite books is *The Art of Gathering* by Priya Parker, and it changed the way I will think about meetings forever. It helped me embrace the idea of being a host at work. If you're being a great host, no one should ever feel uncomfortable or uncertain about what they can expect when they arrive.

Of course, this is not to say that you can't ever be spontaneous, but a social gathering that has planned entertainment or intentional pairings of people feels so much more meaningful than those parties where you stand around with a drink in your hand, bouncing from one batch of awkward small talk to the next.

Are *You* the Drama?

I framed this habit as though other people are the energy vampires and the cause of chaos in your calendar, but sometimes we have to admit, as one of my favorite Taylor Swift lyrics says, "Hi, I'm the problem, it's me." Remember Marie, the luxury interior designer who paid off her credit card debt? She realized that she had a habit of overbooking her calendar, leading to pure exhaustion and feeling overwhelmed about all the tasks she had on her plate.

She texted me one day when she realized she'd messed up. She had spent over a week at an interior design conference, and because she'd been out for so long, she had scheduled herself for back-to-back client meetings the minute she got back. She felt unprepared and anxious, and instead of telling her to push through her meetings, I suggested that she take a deep breath...and reschedule all the meetings that she could.

If you are going to show up to a meeting where you're too exhausted, it's better for you and the other parties to reschedule for a time when you can show up as the best version of yourself. This was hard for her because she doesn't like disappointing people, but it turned out that three of her four meetings were happy to reschedule. She was able to use the day to regroup and re-energize so she could show up even more prepared for them. I'm super proud of Marie because, as one of my long-standing clients and now close friends, I've seen her grow from employee to six-figure self-employed entrepreneur!

The Drama Drain means that when you send communications, they are clear and concise and are as effective as having a meeting itself. I have several CRUSH Bootcamp members who I call "recovering corporate robots"; they spend so much time crafting emails and PowerPoint presentations and meeting minutes that they don't have time or energy for actual critical-thinking tasks. For my business-coaching clients, I spend a lot of time teaching them just how to get straight to the point—without sounding like a jerk.

The Drama Drain means that if you are the one requesting to "pick someone's brain," you first ask yourself whether you're asking someone to spend their precious time on things you could find through your own research, or if you're really invested in following through. I talk to many thought leaders who have felt the frustration of eagerly sharing their mentorship for free, often at the expense of paid time or time with loved ones, only to have that person completely ghost them!

SCHEDULING FOR SELF-NOURISHMENT CAN HELP YOU EXECUTE YOUR MONEY GOALS

Whenever I share my strict calendaring habit with new CRUSH Bootcamp members, they often assume that it's restrictive rather than liberating. Like an effective budget requires allocating funds wisely, you also need a clear calendar to allocate time toward taking care of your physical and mental health.

Before I practiced a regular budgeting routine and the Drama Drain, I worked fifty hours or more a week and then would only schedule any health-related appointments when I was well into burnout symptoms.

When I started to plan my personal-care expenses alongside my basic ones, I learned I could afford them even though they felt luxurious as long as I scheduled them at the beginning of the month, rather than ad hoc. Scheduling them early in my month ensured that I would prioritize these appointments before I spent money on impulse purchases. Now I allocate at least 25% of my monthly budget toward healthy activities that revive me, including physical therapy and mental health counseling. Those items are nonnegotiable—both on my budget and my schedule. By prioritizing self-nourishment in your budget in conjunction with your calendar, you can practice financial freedom long before you hit your independence number.

The Drama Drain means that when you look at your calendar, you're enthused about what you will accomplish and who you will cross paths with that week. It also means that you're not scheduled every minute of every day. It means that you have actual white space to be spontaneous or just to rest. What does this have to do with your money plan? Absolutely everything! Remember, financial freedom is not about the numbers alone. The true test of freedom is when you can look at how you spend your life as moments you got to choose out of joy and not out of obligation.

RICH REFLECTIONS

Review your calendar for this week. Are there meetings that could be a waste of your time? Can you cancel them or turn them into emails instead? Does that feel hard for you? Why?

How many colors do you need to identify the different types of energy you use each week? How can you best arrange your various types of energy throughout the week?

Are there upcoming meetings or gatherings that you're not excited about? Why not? Do you still have to go? If you do have to go, how can you turn it into a more enthusiastic yes?

Are there any energy vampires that you need to bless and release? How would your financial-freedom plan benefit from letting them go?

What challenges do you anticipate in keeping the Drama Drain as a habit going forward? Who do you need to communicate these boundaries to in order to keep your calendar drama-free?

THE PEACE PLAN:
Talk Money with Your Family

As a financial coach, I often work with adults in the "sandwich generation" who are stressed out not only about their own financial responsibilities for themselves and their kids but for their parents as well. In particular, I work with many people in communities of color who feel it's their moral obligation to act as their parents' retirement plan, even if they don't feel financially stable themselves.

If you expect that you might have some obligation to help your elders in their retirement, I beg you to start the habit of what I call the Peace Plan sooner rather than later. Specifically, having the tough conversations at least once a year with your elders about how their finances might impact yours. There are a lot of money wounds that are interlinked with intergenerational wealth and can lead to intergenerational trauma if money conversations with your parents aren't normalized.

Let's outline the specific steps you can take to make this overlooked habit into your Peace Plan.

Don't Assume Your Parents Know or Care about Money in the Same Way You Do

My father passed away in May 2021 and up until recently, I kept reopening the money wound that "no one taught me about how to manage money." I hear the same response from many of the people I've coached—that they had no financial literacy education while growing up.

It only occurred to me recently that my parents *couldn't* teach me how to manage money well because they were already doing the best they could as immigrants who left rural areas of a developing nation to build families, careers, and stable homes completely from scratch. I resolved to stop resenting my parents for what they did not have the capacity to teach me. When I started managing my money well, I'm not proud to say that I was obnoxious about it. I brought up what I learned in family gatherings, sent financial books as gifts, and scoffed when asked why we were being so "cheap."

Eventually, I just had to mind my own business and stop offering unsolicited advice. You can't and shouldn't try to heal other people's money wounds when they never asked you to. Instead of just pushing your own financial beliefs onto the people you love, start by listening to what really worries them and open the conversation if they let you know they are ready to receive it.

Pursue Your Own Financial Independence Before Helping Others

I once was criticized for pursuing financial independence because it appears to be selfish. People who want financial independence are often perceived as caring for just themselves instead of others.

When my husband and I paid off all that debt and I quit my corporate job to pursue my own business, my in-laws started taking notice and asking questions. I shared our net worth, our budget, and how our "cheap" choices were allowing us to take more time off from work. To my surprise, my in-laws accelerated their mortgage payments and paid off their house shortly after we paid off ours. I was surprised since it felt like they hadn't been listening all along. It turned out that showing them, rather than telling them, was much more effective.

Many of my students have voiced similar concerns, particularly those from collectivist cultures who feel guilty for prioritizing their own finances before those of their families. I've had several Filipino students who send money back to their families in the Philippines, even when deep in their own debt and living paycheck to paycheck.

Financially supporting aging parents when your own finances are unsustainable can only last so long. It took my husband and me three years to pay off $300,000 of debt, but in exchange, we can now afford to take care of ourselves and our parents if we need to. Pursuing your own financial independence first will ultimately create not only more generational wealth but also more freedom to spend money with your family while you are all still alive and well.

Don't Leave Your Parents' Expectations Unspoken, Even If It's Uncomfortable

Even though I've been married into my husband's family for thirteen years, for most of that time AJ and I never discussed our parents' retirement plans, and I was afraid from the experience with my mom's health condition and my father's passing that we may be on the hook for their unexpected expenses.

Although I knew it would be a challenging conversation, a few years ago I resolved that we would try and find out what both sides of our families were expecting from us in terms of financial support in their retirement years. I started the conversation in an upbeat manner, sharing my excitement for them to enjoy their retirement after decades of hard work, and I let them know I wanted to see how we could help them.

In that first conversation with each side of our family, there were points where we agreed and points where we didn't. Rather than try to resolve them in that first meeting, I simply took notes on what was said so that we could work on it over time. Not pressuring myself to have a solution to all the problems made it easier to have the conversation in the first place. The point of this conversation was for me to at least understand their intent, rather than know every piece of logistics.

For example, I learned that my mom expected money to be sent to her family in the Philippines, which we had never discussed before. I took note of that, without getting stressed out about the fact that I didn't know how much or to whom this money would go. I let her know we would resolve those details at another time. This was about plans and personal preference, not about financial education. This was about making sure nothing was left unsaid.

CRUSH BOOTCAMP *Success* **STORY**

Are Your Parents Afraid of Retirement?

Many of my CRUSH Bootcamp members are part of the aforementioned "sandwich generation," and just as much as they ask questions for their kids, they ask questions about how to handle their parents. I shared with my CRUSH Bootcamp that I struggled in helping my own family manage their fears around retirement. When my mother-in-law started contemplating retirement, I asked what was stopping her. I learned she was scared to retire, when I had assumed she would be excited. Despite having a financial planner for many years, my in-laws weren't sure if they had enough to retire. My mother-in-law's fear wasn't without reason. Federal Reserve data shows the median balance in a retirement account in 2019 for a household nearing retirement (age 55 to 64) was just $144,000.

At first, I was frustrated she hadn't shared this fear sooner. I then realized it was less about hiding finances from us and more about the shame of having worked hard for so many years and still thinking they hadn't saved enough.

Even more surprisingly, she had no idea what she wanted to do in retirement. It saddened me to hear her say, "If I'm not working, what good am I?" I witnessed my father have that same loss of identity when he retired. He spent years looking for new things to do and things that would make him feel like he was still valuable. I hadn't considered that she was conditioned to think, like so many of our parents were, that working equals worth.

I learned my mother-in-law likes going to Broadway shows, and so we've made it a regular family gathering. Since then, my husband and I have had more frequent conversations with his parents. The great news is that they've been retired for a few years now and are getting more comfortable spending money toward travel and fun. We're encouraging them to explore new interests and hobbies and spending more time with them than we did in the past.

After I shared this story with the CRUSH Bootcamp, several members were encouraged to speak to their own parents about their financial statuses, not out of frustration but rather with empathy. It's often hard to remember that our parents are humans too. Realizing their parents had many of the same fears around money that they did, a few of the CRUSH Bootcamp members acknowledged that they needed to approach their frustrations with their families with greater care.

Write Down the Questions You Need Answered to Feel at Peace

I found myself worrying about the financial obligations of caretaking sooner than my friends did, especially because I knew that in Filipino culture, I was implicitly expected to take care of my parents, even if I couldn't afford it. I am the eighth of my father's nine children. He was older than most of my peers' parents, and my mother was plagued with various health issues that forced her to leave the workforce earlier than expected.

I had no idea where to begin, so I started by simply writing down the questions I had for them:

- Do you owe any money? Are you planning to pay your debts down?
- What amount do you have saved for retirement?
- How much is on the mortgage? Are you planning to stay in this home?
- If there's a health emergency, what is your expectation of me? Of my siblings?
- Would you want to go to an assisted living facility?
- What do you think about having an aide come to your home?

The swirl of questions in my head gave me a lot of anxiety because I realized how little I knew about my parents' financial position and how costly it could be to care for elderly parents. Getting the questions out of my brain and onto paper helped me organize my thoughts and helped facilitate a conversation with my husband about what questions he had for his parents too.

Have Your Own Estate Plan, Even If You're Young and Healthy

I unfortunately had to learn the hard way what it's like to have someone pass away with no plan in place. When my father died, we were left to make a lot of financial decisions while also managing grief.

Two out of three Americans do not have any type of estate planning document, according to a study by Caring.com. It's uncomfortable, but

I found that creating my own estate plan not only helped me feel more financially responsible, it also equipped me to have a more informed conversation with my aging parents, who didn't have anything in place.

Even though we are relatively young and healthy, my husband and I review our estate plan annually, or whenever our assets have changed significantly, like after we sold our house. It's an annual reminder to review all our assets and insurances but also to have a deeper review about the relationships that matter to us most. An estate plan can feel overwhelming, so here's where you can at least start with the basics:

- An asset inventory, including real estate, bank accounts, investments, and personal property (all of which you can derive from your net worth tracker)
- Contact information for your attorneys, financial advisors, accountants, and key family members
- A specific location where you will keep all your important documents so someone will know where to find them
- Updated beneficiaries for your accounts and policies, including retirement accounts, life insurance policies, and other accounts that have beneficiary designations
- A letter of intent that provides specific instructions that may not be legally binding but can guide the people you love to know what you wanted without having to read your mind

Having our own estate plans also gave us a path to talk about finances with our families because we were walking the walk and not just talking when it came to planning for the future. In hindsight, I wish I had spoken about our own finances with my family much sooner. But now we habitually talk about money openly, and my in-laws feel more comfortable asking money questions because we shared details with them first.

RICH REFLECTIONS

How familiar are you with your parents' current financial situation, including their retirement savings and any outstanding debts?

Have you begun gathering important documentation related to your parents' estate planning, such as wills, insurance policies, and investment accounts? If not, what's preventing you from starting this process?

What questions do you have for your parents regarding their financial obligations, such as mortgage payments, healthcare costs, and potential long-term care plans?

Have you considered how your parents feel about retirement beyond the financial aspect, such as their emotional readiness and post-retirement goals?

In what ways have you demonstrated financial independence and responsibility to your parents, and how do you want to influence their financial decisions or perceptions?

THE MONTHLY MEETUP:
Find Your CRUSH Community

We've got it backward, y'all. Money isn't precious; it's time that is. Money is the means, not the end. If you want to start feeling any sense of financial freedom, it's crucial to stop using time to buy money and instead use money to buy time. However, a personal money wound I am still working on healing is what I call toxic productivity. It's the idea that if I'm not busy all the time, I must be worthless. If I'm not making as much money as possible, my life must be less valuable.

For as long as I can remember, my father would refer to people by their job titles rather than by their characteristics or his fondness of them. One of his eight siblings was coming to visit from the Philippines, and I asked my father to tell me about him and his family. He told me my uncle's job and my aunt's job, which, to my father, was a big deal as they were quite successful. I told my father that I asked who they were, not what their jobs were—but to him, that information was one and the same. That brother and my father both passed away during the COVID-19 pandemic, and at our family gatherings to honor them, no one talked about their jobs.

Find Your People

That experience got me to realize that all the time we spend making money will likely be forgotten. It's all the time we spend loving and laughing and living that will be remembered. But it's hard to keep that perspective when you've got bills to pay and you're trying to break that paycheck-to-paycheck cycle! And even if you've reached a certain level of financial security, I can personally attest that it's really challenging to escape the fear that if you're not working hard, you don't have enough money. That's why this last habit I'll share with you is to find your CRUSH community and meet with them monthly at the very least. Your CRUSH community is the handful of people who will not only root for you in building the habits outlined under CRUSH, but they'll be willing to run the race alongside you.

Now, I have an actual formal membership called the CRUSH Boot-camp where I host regular monthly meetings for people following the CRUSH steps, provide mentorship and guidance, and share wins and challenges with empathetic people. We meet over Zoom with people from all around the world! I've recently started to host more in-person gatherings, and my heart always feels so full after I meet with my members.

Keep in mind that your closest friends might not be the people who are best suited to be your partners in financial matters. First and foremost, look for people who are striving for freedom and are motivated to make changes, and see if they'd like to meet periodically to keep one another accountable, share ideas, and provide encouragement.

In my opinion, there's no such thing as a self-made millionaire. Everyone I've ever met who has become independently wealthy had people supporting them in different ways. You can't do this alone. Well, I suppose you could, but wow, how boring would that be?

Instead, I want you to seek out a supportive group of people who are also interested in financial freedom and being a bit contrarian in their money habits and beliefs. So many of us grew up in households where that abundance mentality wasn't available, and it's much easier to build that mindset when you've got other people to model it for you. Here are my best tips on making your own CRUSH community into a monthly habit worth keeping.

Learn from Friends Ten Years Ahead and Behind You

You can't predict the future, but you can learn from people who have already been where you want to go. In my journey toward financial independence and early retirement, I've benefited from the financial perspectives of CRUSH Bootcamp members and peers in their forties and fifties and not just my peers in their thirties like me.

One of the best side effects of having a membership like this is that we have multiple generations represented in our current group. Our youngest is in their twenties and the oldest is in her seventies! If you only surround yourself with people in your own age group, you miss out on the rich perspectives of generations and periods of time you wouldn't have experienced yourself. I have several CRUSH Bootcamp members who are pursuing vastly different careers in their fifties, and they remind me it's never too late to start investing in yourself and your future. And I love that they're always willing to share their wisdom with the younger members. I had a CRUSH Bootcamp member named Deb who turned age seventy-two the year I am writing this book. She found me through a membership she joined at which I was a guest speaker and now refers to me as her Auntie B, despite being more than thirty years my senior. She said, "I think this is important for me to share with everybody. I have no end of thank-yous for Bernadette and AJ for coming out and doing this work because it's helped enormously. But it's still taking time. It just takes time. And it's going to be different rates for us. We have to be patient with ourselves as long as we keep going."

I'm forever grateful to her because she stayed in my programs beyond the required ninety days and remained enthusiastic and encouraging to everyone in the group. She and so many others remind me the financial journey is hard, but you don't have to do it alone. And it's so much more fun when you do it alongside people who truly believe in financial freedom.

I often feel like I'm behind financially when I compare myself to ambitious twenty-year-olds who became stars in the startup and content creator worlds. But almost all of my older friends tell me they wish they had done what I did and invested much earlier, quit earlier, or started something earlier. Comparing yourself to others and stressing about what you didn't do is dangerous, so just remember to celebrate wherever you are in your own journey, because yours is a path that no one else will ever repeat!

And let's not discount the younger folks, please! I am constantly in awe of how Gen Z learns so quickly, is so comfortable with technology, and isn't afraid to stand up for social causes they believe in. One of my younger CRUSH Bootcamp members is awesome at sharing about up-and-coming trendsetters in the personal finance space who she follows, and so I get to learn from them too! For example, there was a recent trend called "loud budgeting," which Gen Z coined, where people encouraged one another to be loud and proud about being on a budget! I later wrote several articles about how that trend could encourage millennials and older generations to be more honest about their finances with their friends.

Attract a Millionaire Money Mentor Who Represents Your Values

Several of my CRUSH Bootcamp members are people who initially started following me on social media and eventually reached out to ask me for guidance in a genuine and thoughtful manner, not just to "pick my brain." Here's what not to do when you are looking for a real money mentor, specifically someone who is likely already busy and gets these requests often:

Don't

- Ask them for advice that requires them to know you personally. For example, asking "What should I invest in?" to a stranger is a bad question because it's highly dependent on the person.
- Ask them for information that is already publicly shared online. For example, I often have people ask me how I started my business, when with a quick google search you can find tons of articles on how I did that.
- Ask someone to meet for coffee if you've never met them before. Instead, you may try asking for responses via email to start off with and see if an in-person conversation is warranted later.

The best way for you to attract a millionaire money mentor is to exude the energy and confidence that you'll one day be a millionaire too! Here are a few tips on what you should do if you want to attract a real money mentor who will invest in you:

Do

- Show genuine interest in their work. Cite an article or an accomplishment they had and let them know how it inspired you.
- Ask for resources more than advice. Find out what tools, books, podcasts, or memberships they found most beneficial instead of asking for "life advice."
- Offer to pay them. I've seen more often than not that they will decline the offer, but they will appreciate the gesture and will know that you won't waste their time.

Your Peers Should Pressure You Positively

The truth is, part of the reason I started CRUSH Your Money Goals is because, selfishly, I wanted more cool women to hang out with once I had more free time myself! In 2024, I held my first "Well-thy Summit," where I gathered twelve of my best CRUSH Bootcamp members to spend two days building our financial-freedom plans together. They came from various parts of the country, and by the end of the weekend they were hugging and demanding follow-ups from one another on the goals they'd set for themselves.

Renee, one of my longest-standing CRUSH Bootcamp members, let it slip that she had enough money to pay down her mortgage and really enter early retirement but was hesitant because of all the traditional advice she'd heard about keeping the debt and investing instead. To my surprise, I didn't have to say a thing, because multiple others spoke out and did all the coaching for me! They encouraged her to consider differently, asked her insightful questions, and cited all the lessons they'd learned through the CRUSH framework.

A few weeks later, she announced to the group that she'd bitten the bullet and paid off her home! The pure joy from these former-strangers-turned-cheerleaders was such an honor for me to witness. And I'm super confident that the years that Renee and I put in together focusing on her financial-freedom plan will have her retired years ahead of schedule.

Using Social Media to Connect Mindfully

Remember the Unsubscribe Button habit from earlier in the book? While I generally stay away from constant comparisons, results from a study published in the *Journal of Behavioral Finance* highlight the potential of a social-comparison approach to motivate individuals to start saving for retirement or increase their current savings when they learn that other people are doing it too. Peer pressure can be positive when it's focused on building wealth, not just flaunting it! By curating your CRUSH community, you can minimize exposure to materialistic influences and instead embrace conversations that encourage financial responsibility. A great place to find these money mentors is social media, if you're looking for people who actually educate and don't just entertain and who you may want to approach as one-on-one mentors in real life. If you want to learn how to become rich, it's best to learn from someone who is actually rich in real life, so be sure to vet them before you believe what they say.

I unfollowed the influencers who were clearly pushing products and replaced them with fellow financial educators who focus on teaching personal finance, real estate savvy, and entrepreneurship. I've now even had the opportunity to meet many of these women in real life. We can share resources, and I'm genuinely happy to see them succeed. Many might think that they're my competitors, but I truly believe there's enough room for all of us. I'm happy to recommend other money mentors who might be better fits for someone if my style or philosophy isn't their cup of tea.

This shift to connecting rather than competing will encourage you to consume narratives and experiences that inspire the development of wealth-building habits as opposed to simply portraying a wealthy lifestyle in comparison to your peers. Specifically, consider personal finance communities featuring individuals who feel relatable and honest, reflecting values important to your cultural heritage and current life stage. Regularly review your membership in these types of communities by asking yourself these questions:

- Are these conversations still relevant to me?
- Am I compelled to engage with the people in the community, not just the leader?
- Am I learning practical tips that I can implement now, not just in the far future?

As a female professional who spent a significant portion of my early career in male-dominated industries, I intentionally sought out female money mentors who are investors, entrepreneurs, and thought leaders. I didn't see female representation reflected in my real-life environment until recently. Representation really matters when you're choosing who to help guide you in your journey!

Watching my parents retire together, I learned you may not want to do everything with just your spouse or kids, or they may not be available when you're ready to explore. Feel free to find people whose financial goals and interests match yours. Meeting with a motivated community of leaders (not just followers) on a monthly basis is a habit that will not only increase your net worth but increase your self-worth by leaps and bounds. Later in this book, I share specific financial educators who I admire and whose communities I recommend you check out. And of course, I'd love for you to consider joining our real-life CRUSH Bootcamp if you've enjoyed reading this book!

RICH REFLECTIONS

Consider the influence of familial attitudes toward work and success on your own mindset. How can you detach your self-worth from your productivity and financial achievements?

Think about a time when positive peer pressure influenced your financial decisions. How did the support of your bootcamp peers impact your mindset or actions regarding money management?

Imagine your ideal support system for achieving financial freedom. Who would be part of your CRUSH Bootcamp, and what qualities would they possess?

Explore the concept of intergenerational learning within your CRUSH Bootcamp. What's one way you can benefit from the wisdom and experiences of older members? Of younger members?

What are three ways you need to evolve in order to attract a supportive community that aligns with your financial goals?

Read This When
You Feel Like Giving Up

Wow! If you made it this far in the book, give yourself a hug right now. No, really—I love hugging myself; it sounds silly but it really works!

With so many other options for content, the fact that you made it here shows that you are serious about pursuing financial independence, and you should be proud of yourself. I credit the CRUSH Bootcamp for revealing that financial evolution takes time, sometimes more than expected. In fact, they're the ones who taught me it's a lifelong pursuit. What initially appeared as a straightforward path morphed into a crooked journey, illustrating the unpredictability of personal finance. Eventually it led to what is now a cycle that represents the five steps repeating themselves over the years as you take on new financial levels in your journey to independence.

Now, I know I just threw a ton of habits and information at you. I told you I'd be lying if I said this process would be easy. Will you likely want to give up and just go back to settling for financial stress? It's likely. That's because staying the same is easy. Committing to change is hard, but necessary if you want to be the boss of your money! So before you give up, let me answer some of your hesitations and frustrations and encourage you to keep going!

Remember this: There are 168 hours in a week, and to build great money habits, you only need to dedicate 5 (max!) of those—that's a mere 3% of your time! Wouldn't you be happy to trade a few hours a week to save decades of financial stress?

Keep in mind that I don't expect that you'll be able to implement *all* of these habits immediately. It took me at least three to six months to turn these strategies into habits I could stick to. If you're challenging yourself with big financial goals this year, even implementing just one of these habits alongside your money plan can make a big difference in your wealth and your health. You don't need all twenty-five habits to happen all at once, so if you want the least amount of analysis paralysis, start with one habit at a time. Sustainability matters more than speed.

All that said, I totally understand that there is a right time for everything. If you're not able to focus on your finances at this level right now, no worries. Committed leaders come back and try again when they're ready, so give yourself permission to do that. Now that you know these habits, they'll percolate in the back of your mind as you continue your journey, and I bet one day you'll be ready to try them.

It's also very normal to lose your motivation from time to time. Here are a few of the most common hesitations or blockers I hear from people just like you and some motivational boosters to keep you on track.

Issue: I'm too emotionally drained to get good with money, but I can't afford weekly therapy. What should I do?

Solution: Try quarterly therapy.

Having strong and consistent mental well-being habits is a big part of a successful financial plan. They help you believe in yourself, overcome challenges, and keep persevering so that you make material progress in your financial goals.

That's why one of the key habits that can change the trajectory of your personal finances and help you become a debt-free millionaire is to shift away from societal norms that view therapy as a luxury or a sign of mental instability. In fact, I recommend that you consider quarterly therapy a part of your long-term investment strategy. Going four times a year will be more manageable in your budget and still provides a lot of benefit.

About 1 in 5 Americans reported getting mental health treatment 2021, but 42% of adults with a diagnosable condition reported in 2023 that they could not afford treatment, according to national nonprofit Mental Health America.

Despite the dominant narrative in my culture as a first-generation Asian American being to avoid therapy, I decided to incorporate regular quarterly appointments with a licensed mental health professional as part of my financial plan, not just my health plan. At first, going to therapy felt both intimidating and expensive because my preferred provider was not covered by insurance and cost more than $200 per session.

Rather than look at therapy as a cost, I chose to consider it a long-term investment the same way I would a retirement account. I figured that though I might not feel the effects of it immediately, the benefits may compound over time.

I committed to trying a session out once every ninety days and set aside that money in my regular budget. Over time, I learned that therapy helped me manage the anxiety and unlearn cultural scripts that have held me back from taking bigger steps in my finances. You will likely experience similar growth.

Issue: I'm too tired! I already work so hard.

Solution: Prioritize sleep!

When I first started having extra cash flow after paying off all my debts, I fell into the clichés of what was touted as self-care for women: pedicures, massages, hair appointments, and charcuterie boards with wine. And yet, I felt no less anxious and no more revitalized. It turned out those practices weren't giving me what I *really* needed: sleep.

According to the Centers for Disease Control and Prevention, about one in three American adults report not getting enough rest or sleep every day. And so I traded out my weekly self-care appointments for blocks of time during which I allowed myself to take a nap or go to a deep-stretch yoga class that was mostly me lying on a body pillow.

Oddly, I felt really guilty adding this to my weekly schedule, because of the consistent narrative I had heard in my years of working in fast-paced industries like finance and tech startups that rest was "lazy." But thanks to blocking off a consistent rest period in my weekly calendar, I've had the great financial side effect of curbing the impulse spending that usually came with feeling exhausted and burned out.

You know what's crazy? The days that I'm super busy and stressed are the days that I now absolutely force myself to go to yoga, dance, meditate, or take a nap. You need rest as a nonnegotiable block of your weekly schedule if you want any shot at financial freedom.

Issue: Hiring a financial coach is too expensive.

Solution: Shift to an investment mentality and make a financial coach a priority.

Elite athletes have coaches even though they're talented and trained. That's because coaches help you achieve your goals in ways you would not be able to do alone. Still, if you checked out my website and your pocket whispered, "Ouch," I feel you! But hey, buckle up because we're talking about an investment in your financial-freedom journey! I promise you, hiring an expert is a plan worth prioritizing in your budget. And if you really can't swing it now, save for it until you can.

Why am I so sure? Here are a few nuggets to noodle on: If your household makes six figures, a coach like me is just asking for a humble 1% of that annual income. That's like the loose change in your financial sofa that'll keep paying off for years to come! More importantly, by the end of this adventure with a skilled coach, you're not just getting a plan—you're getting a whopping $100,000 worth of tangible steps toward financial freedom. Yep, that's a 100x return on your investment for clients who work with me.

But more honestly, the mindset of "I can't afford this" is the actual problem. It's time to swap that expense mentality for an investment mindset. Think gains, not drains! Not all coaches are the same, though, so make sure you vet them carefully if you decide to work with one.

There are a lot of financial coaches, but few are debt-free millionaires, retired early, and will work with you personally. Many peers of mine charge $2,000 per hour just to pick their brain. You should also always

222 Read This When You Feel Like Giving Up

look for a money-back guarantee—making this decision a total no-brainer. A good coach is willing to stand by their results and offer you your money back if they don't deliver what they promised. That will help you make sure this isn't just a cash grab. Your future self will thank you!

If you still feel like you can't afford a money coach right now, you can save up for it and join later—just be prepared the price may be higher. I know a few coaches who had total glow ups, and now people are sad they are priced out!

Issue: My partner isn't on board. What should I do?

Solution: Be patient, but don't wait for them to make your own progress.

Usually when I hear this, it's because a couple isn't using tangible data, just old narratives to argue about money. You need to shift to planning together from a mutual set of facts, not individual emotions. Before I became a financial coach, I strongly believed married couples should absolutely combine all their financial accounts. But after coaching a diverse range of people, I learned there are valid reasons to keep separate accounts even if you are married.

When my husband and I decided to keep all our financial accounts—cash, debts, investments, and properties—in one view using a tool like Monarch Money, the focus became less about what was happening in any particular account. How would we move our joint net worth forward as a team?

Once we had an accurate dashboard for making our financial decisions together, our conversations became less emotional. In other words, our conversations changed from emotionally charged statements like "You always do this" to more objective observations like "Our trends show that our spending looks like this."

Whether you keep separate checking accounts or credit cards or not, you can still provide visibility into each other's accounts without necessarily exerting unsolicited opinions or judgments over how your partner might choose to spend.

Employing the ideas I outline in this book took AJ and me years to learn and eventually convert into habits. If you and your partner are not on the same page right away, give yourselves a calendar year before you give up. With both of you likely operating from years of different financial backgrounds, beliefs, and styles, it's only natural that it will take several months of practice to shift your financial plan toward retiring early together.

Issue: Is it too late for me? Am I too old?

Solution: No! The best time to start is now.

Guess what? The money train doesn't care about age—hop on board anytime, because you're never too old to rock the money game! I've coached so many fabulous alumni who hit their financial primes in their fifties, sixties, and seventies and turned their net worth into six or seven figures.

The question should be: Why wait any longer? Your money's been itching to work its magic for you, and it's time to give it the stage it deserves! Don't let time slip away—kick off that journey to financial independence with a bang!

I'm super grateful to you for taking precious hours of your life to read this book. I hope this book travels with you throughout your lifetime, and I hope that I can maybe even meet you in real life someday to give you a big hug!

Your millionaire mentor,
Bernadette Joy

Ten Amazing Female Personal Finance Experts to Follow

I don't believe in competition. There's room for all of us! Benefit from getting a diversity of opinions when it comes to money from experts who are fun, engaging, and real. Here are some amazing women in personal finance who have helped me grow in my personal finance journey and who can help you too! (In alphabetical order by last name.)

Marsha Barnes

Helps women and couples achieve financial wellness through financial therapy, education, and an innovative learning hub on wheels.
https://thefinancebar.com

Yanely Espinal

Stage speaker, financial educator, and author.
https://missbehelpful.com

Stefanie Gonzales

Investing and career consultant (and my podcast cohost!).
https://instagram.com/womenswealtheffect/?hl=en

Giovanna "Gigi" Gonzalez

Teaches financial literacy and career readiness to first-generation Latinas.

https://thefirstgenmentor.com

Shang Saavedra

National personal finance and retirement expert.

https://savemycents.com

Jamila Souffrant

Host of the *Journey to Launch* podcast.

https://jamilasouffrant.com

Farnoosh Torabi

American personal finance expert, journalist, author, and television personality.

https://farnoosh.tv

Jannese Torres

Host of the *Yo Quiero Dinero* podcast, a platform to connect listeners with Latinx and POC change makers in money.

https://yoquierodineropodcast.com

Mandi Woodruff-Santos

Career coach, personal finance expert, speaker, writer, and cohost of the *Brown Ambition* podcast.

https://mandimoney.com

Cindy Zuniga-Sanchez

Author, speaker, and lawyer.

https://zero-basedbudget.com

My Recommended Resources

Please note that some of these resources are affiliate URLs (notated with a *), which means I may earn a commission if you make a purchase through these URLs. Please note that I only recommend products that I personally use and believe will add value to my readers. Your support helps keep this content affordable for our CRUSH Bootcamp community. Thank you for your understanding and support!

Monarch Money*

This is a net worth tracker (US based) and is my favorite way to track my net worth and all my accounts for a nominal fee each month.

https://monarchmoney.com/referral/dh9y5g51d4

Empower

Use this free and secure net worth tool to see your true net worth in real time. It's free because it is linked to an investment firm, so you may receive ads or invitations to join their services, however don't feel pressured to!

https://empower.com/personal-investors/net-worth

EveryDollar

I've used this tool consistently for eight years at the time of writing this book. I've never used the paid version and it has everything I need in the free version.

https://everydollar.com

Compound Interest Calculator

The US Securities and Exchange Commission offers a free compound interest calculator that helps you determine how much your money can grow using the power of compound interest.

https://investor.gov/financial-tools-calculators/calculators/compound-interest-calculator

Fidelity Investments

My go-to investment platform for my individual retirement accounts and taxable investing.

https://fidelity.com

Guideline

I switched 401(k) providers to Guideline for their easy-to-navigate funds and simple dashboard. They now offer IRAs too.

https://guideline.com

Discover Bank

Where I personally bank thanks to their excellent customer service and easy-to-use online platform.

https://discover.com/online-banking/

Kajabi*

If you have a knowledge-based business or want to start one, this is the best system. I use it to run my six-figure business and have made over $700,000 since 2020!

https://kajabi.com/?utm_campaign=home_trial&utm_content=71447&utm_medium=affiliate&utm_source=Bernadette+Joy+Cruz+Maulion

Selected Sources

Chapter 3

Bankrate: "Bankrate's 2024 Annual Emergency Savings Report"

https://bankrate.com/banking/savings/emergency-savings-report/
#rising-prices

US Bureau of Labor Statistics: "Consumer Expenditures—2022"

https://bls.gov/news.release/cesan.nr0.htm

Zippia: "40 Important Job Interview Statistics [2023]: How Many Interviews Before Job Offer"

https://zippia.com/advice/job-interview-statistics/

Forbes Advisor: "How to Create an Emergency Fund"

https://forbes.com/advisor/banking/how-to-create-an-emergency-fund/

Forbes Advisor: "What Is the Average Credit Card Interest Rate This Week?"

https://forbes.com/advisor/credit-cards/average-credit-card-interest-rate/

Forbes Advisor: "Credit Card Interest Calculator"

https://forbes.com/advisor/credit-cards/credit-card-interest-calculator/

Experian: "Average Credit Card Debt Increases 10% to $6,501 in 2023"

https://experian.com/blogs/ask-experian/state-of-credit-cards/

PYMNTS: "Gen Z, Millennials Use Credit Cards 30% More Than the Average Cardholder"

https://pymnts.com/credit-cards/2023/gen-z-millennials-use-credit-cards-30-more-than-the-average-cardholder/

MIT Sloan Experts, Behavioral Science: "How Credit Cards Activate the Reward Center of Our Brains and Drive Spending"

https://mitsloan.mit.edu/experts/how-credit-cards-activate-reward-center-our-brains-and-drive-spending

Journal of Consumer Research: "'Paper or Plastic?': How We Pay Influences Post-Transaction Connection"

https://academic.oup.com/jcr/article-abstract/42/5/688/1857957?redirectedFrom=fulltext

FICO: "What's in My FICO® Scores?"

https://myfico.com/credit-education/whats-in-your-credit-score

Forbes: "Why Your Budget Plan Isn't Working—and 5 Ways to Fix It Fast"

https://forbes.com/sites/bernadettejoy/2023/05/05/why-your-budget-plan-isnt-working---and-5-ways-to-fix-it-fast/

Chapter 4

Forbes Advisor: "Living Paycheck to Paycheck Statistics 2024"

https://forbes.com/advisor/banking/living-paycheck-to-paycheck-statistics-2024/

Forbes: "I Paid Off $300,000 of Debt in 3 Years. These 3 Habits Made the Difference"

https://forbes.com/sites/bernadettejoy/2023/05/25/i-paid-off-300000-of-debt-in-3-years--heres-3-money-habits-to-start-today/

Forbes: "Use This Investing Formula to Reach Financial Freedom in Retirement"

https://forbes.com/sites/bernadettejoy/2023/11/29/use-this-investing-formula-to-reach-financial-freedom-in-retirement/

Chapter 5

Bankrate: "73% of Aspiring Homeowners Cite Affordability As Their Primary Obstacle"

https://bankrate.com/mortgages/homeownership-remains-centerpiece-of-american-dream/

Realtor.com: "The Cities Where You'll Save Money Renting in 2023—and the Ones Where Buying a Home Is Cheaper"

https://realtor.com/news/trends/rent-vs-buy-cities-where-monthly-costs-for-each-are-less/

Pew Research Center: "Gender Pay Gap in US Hasn't Changed Much in Two Decades"

https://pewresearch.org/short-reads/2023/03/01/gender-pay-gap-facts/

Forbes: "Women of Color Set Lower Salary Requirements Than White Men, According to Job Search Site"

https://forbes.com/sites/kimelsesser/2023/02/06/women-of-color-set-lower-salary-requirements-than-white-men-according-to-job-search-site/

Columbia Business School: "New Research Shows That Asking for a Precise—Not Round—Number During Negotiations Can Give You the Upper Hand"

https://business.columbia.edu/press-releases/cbs-press-releases/new-research-shows-asking-precise-not-round-number-during/

Chapter 6

Forbes Advisor: "5 Lessons from Smart Credit Card Maximizers"

https://forbes.com/advisor/credit-cards/lessons-from-credit-card-maximizers/

Forbes Advisor: "2024 Student Loan Debt Statistics: Average Student Loan Debt"

https://forbes.com/advisor/student-loans/average-student-loan-statistics/

Forbes: "20 Facts and Figures to Know When Marketing to Women"

https://forbes.com/sites/forbescontentmarketing/2019/05/13/
20-facts-and-figures-to-know-when-marketing-to-women/

Forbes Advisor: "What Is a 401(k) Match?"

https://forbes.com/advisor/retirement/what-is-401k-match/

Engage with Me Anytime!

CRUSH Your Money Goals Bootcamp

Get personally mentored by me on your financial-freedom plan with challenges, an amazing accountability group, and a personalized plan for your unique situation.

https://crushyourmoneygoals.com

Take a Free Money Masterclass with Me!

Sign up to learn live with me from anywhere in the world in my highly acclaimed money classes, where you can ask me questions in real time!

https://crushyourmoneygoals.com/masterclass

CRUSH Your Money Goals YouTube Channel

Subscribe for weekly videos on all things money and a peek into the behind the scenes of my global travel as a speaker and financial educator!

https://youtube.com/c/bernadettejoy

The *CRUSH Your Money Goals* Podcast

With over sixty episodes, you can follow along for practical tips and inspirational stories to become a millionaire alongside me and my cohost Stefanie Gonzales.

https://podcasts.apple.com/us/podcast/crush-your-money-goals/id1422564669

Social Media

Tag me when posting about your financial-freedom progress and what you learned from this book on your favorite social media channel!

https://instagram.com/bernadebtjoy

https://linkedin.com/in/bernadebtjoy

Grab My Free Guide!

Subscribe to my weekly newsletter to get your free money workbook and get tips from me each week on how to save, invest, and grow your income!

www.crushyourmoneygoals.com/freeguide

Index